The Interactive
Gruesome and GROSS FACTS

igloobooks

igloobooks

Published in 2013
by Igloo Books Ltd
Cottage Farm
Sywell
NN6 0BJ
www.igloobooks.com

SHE001 0713
2 4 6 8 10 9 7 5 3 1
ISBN 978-1-78197-543-5

Printed and manufactured in China

CONTENTS

DINOSAURS

BEASTLY CREATURES

PESKY PLANTS

BULGY BODIES

HISTORY'S HORRORS

STRANGE CUSTOMS

FREAKY FOODS

MEDICAL MATTERS

GHOULISH MONSTERS

DEADLY DISASTERS

INDEX

Interactive Instructions

On your mobile, or tablet device, download the **FREE** Layar App.

Look out for the **SCAN ME** logo and scan the whole page.

Unlock, discover and enjoy the enhanced content.

Available on the iPhone
App Store

Google play

For more details, visit: **www.igloobooks.com**

layar

DINOSAURS

The prehistoric world of dinosaurs must have been a terrifying place, full of the most gruesome and gross sights. There would have been battling monsters tearing and scratching each other apart, and the sound of roaring and stamping would have rent the air.

FOSSIL HUNT

Scientists have been able to recreate the lost world of dinosaurs from fossils and other clues that the huge creatures left behind millions of years ago. From fossils they can work out, for example, how big a dinosaur was, what it ate, what it looked like and even how it might have behaved.

BATTLING IT OUT

Picture an Earth inhabited by feathered reptiles with teeth, giant crocodiles, ocean reptiles as big as whales and small, fast-running dinosaurs hunting in packs. In the battle for survival, hunters and hunted fought with teeth, claws, tail clubs and tail spikes, and some had armored skin.

As well as fossilized bones, dinosaurs left behind fossilized eggs, tracks and footprints that give us extra vital clues as to how they lived.

DOOMED TO DIE OUT

Many prehistoric animals were bigger and fiercer than any animals that have ever lived. Others were small, agile and probably smart. But they were doomed to become extinct, their places taken by species better able to adapt to the ever-changing environment.

7

TERRIFYING TYRANNOSAURUS

The ferocious *Tyrannosaurus* (say tih-RAN-oh-SAWR-us) lived 70 to 65 million years ago. Nothing was safe from its fearsome teeth.

AMAZING!

EGGZACTLY

Like all dinosaurs, *Tyrannosaurus* would have emerged from an egg, probably laid in a nest. Although no *Tyrannosaurus* nests have yet been found, it is thought the eggs would have been relatively small. Baby dinosaurs were able to run as soon as they hatched, so they could escape from predators.

DINOSAUR KING

Tyrannosaurus lived throughout what is now western North America. This monster dinosaur weighed 6.8 tonnes (7.5 tons) – slightly more than the largest African elephant today – and measured about 12.3 m (40 ft) from its nose to the tip of its tail.

SHORT ARMS

Tyrannosaurus ran on its strong back legs. For such a huge beast, its front arms were puny – hardly long enough to help the dinosaur keep its balance. Some experts think that as a baby *Tyrannosaurus* may have had four legs the same size, and that as the rest of the animal grew, its front legs stayed the same size.

BIG HEAD!

Tyrannosaurus's skull measured 1.5 m (5 ft) long, and was a battering ram of bone and teeth. *Tyrannosaurus* would smash its head against its prey and then rip the creature apart. It got its meals by ambushing other dinosaurs or scavenging already-dead creatures.

KILLER TEETH

Tyrannosaurus had a mouthful of the biggest teeth of any dinosaur, and the strongest bite – 15 times stronger than the bite of an African lion. It used its longest teeth (up to 30 cm/12 in. long) to bite off huge chunks of flesh. If a tooth was lost, broken or old, it fell out and a sharp new one took its place.

DID YOU KNOW?

BIG APPETITE

Tyrannosaurus could probably eat as much as 230 kg (500 lb) of meat in one bite (that's as many as 2,000 quarter-pound burgers!). It couldn't use its fingers, though, because its arms were too short to reach up to its mouth. It just bit and swallowed.

VICIOUS RAPTORS

Raptors were hunting dinosaurs, also known as dromaeosaurs or "swift lizards." Some were the size of a wolf, while others were up to 9 m (30 ft) long, and they were vicious.

COOL FACT!

FEATHERED FIEND

Fast-running raptors had feathers like a bird, but they couldn't fly. Instead they ran on their long, scaly legs and seized prey with their vicious claws. Some scientists think that dromaeosaurs and modern birds share a common ancestor. The term "raptor" is also used to describe eagles and other birds of prey with long talons.

Deinonychus (say die-NON-ih-kuss) may have hunted in packs, with more than one of them leaping onto their victim and pinning it to the ground. The prey would have been torn to shreds by their vicious, curved claws.

VELOCIRAPTOR

Many dromaeosaurs could run and climb, and none was more deadly and agile than little *Velociraptor* (say vel-OSS-ih-rap-tore). This "swift thief" lived about 70 million years ago. About the size of a turkey, it would dash up to prey, slash with its razor-sharp claws, skip back out of reach and then attack again.

UTAHRAPTOR

Measuring about 7 m (23 ft) long, *Utahraptor* (say YOU-tah-RAP-tore) was a giant among raptors. This North American killer weighed up to 680 kg (1,500 lb). It had extra-long hooked claws on its feet that it used to rip open the tough hide of its prey. *Utahraptor* roamed the Earth more than 100 million years ago.

SUPER CLAW

Raptors had vicious claws like the talons of an eagle, but much bigger. The "attack-claw" was used like a dagger. It's likely that the raptor leaped into the air, striking downward to tear wounds in the body of its prey. One fossilized *Velociraptor* was found locked in mortal combat with a *Protoceratops* (say PRO-toe-SER-ah-tops), a small, plant-eating dinosaur. The two dinosaurs were probably killed by a collapsing sand dune, or were buried by a sandstorm.

ANOTHER KILLER CARNIVORE

Allosaurus (say al-oh-SAWR-us) was a mighty killer carnivore that prowled the Earth 155 to 135 million years ago.

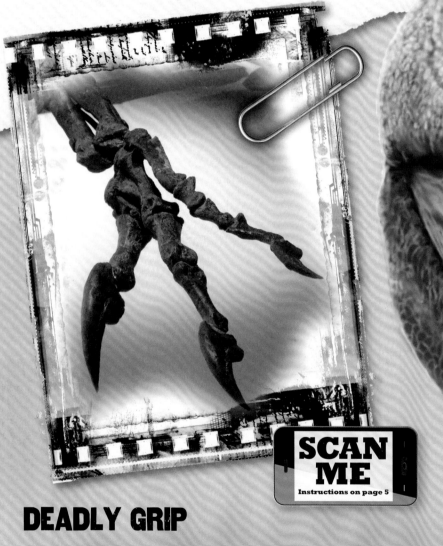

SCAN ME
Instructions on page 5

DEADLY GRIP

Allosaurus lived before the mighty *Tyrannosaurus*. With a big head, powerful back legs and short arms, it was up to 12 m (39 ft) long – twice the length of the biggest great white sharks today. Savage saw-teeth were set in a massive, gaping jaw, and it had sharp claws on its front and back legs.

BLOODY BATTLES

Allosaurus did not need to run fast to hunt its prey – enormous, slow-moving plant-eaters. Battles between such cumbersome prehistoric monsters were probably noisy, brutal and quick. *Allosaurus* would charge open-jawed and kicking, and would gash gaping wounds in its victim before finally killing it.

AMAZING!

AGGRESSIVE

Young allosaurs kept clear of *Allosaurus* adults, which were very aggressive. If several adults met over a kill, it's likely a fight would break out and the loser would end up on the menu!

DINO POOP

A piece of fossilized dino poop is called a coprolite. Millions of years old and rock-hard, coprolites contain traces of the things that dinosaurs ate, such as fish bones, and these give scientists clues as to how the dinosaurs lived. The biggest fossil dino poop is a lump measuring over 60 cm (23 in.) long!

SPIKES AND CLUBS

To fight off predators, some dinosaurs had a tail armed with spikes or a bony club. Being struck by such a weapon could knock an enemy out cold!

STEGOSAURUS

Stegosaurus (say STEG-uh-SAWR-us) was a large, heavily built dinosaur about the size of a bus (8–9 m/26–29.5 ft long), but with a brain the size of a walnut. It lumbered about looking for low-growing plants to eat. On its back were two rows of bony plates, possibly used to intimidate enemies, attract mates or to regulate body temperature.

VICIOUS TAIL SPIKES

If confronted by the fearsome teeth of *Allosaurus* or another meat-eater, *Stegosaurus* would strike its enemy with its spiked tail, ripping out its enemy's eyes and slicing through flesh and muscles. Each spike measured 60–90 cm (2–3 ft) long.

ANKYLOSAURUS

Ankylosaurus (say ANG-ki-lo-SAWR-us) resembled a modern armadillo, but at 7–10 m (23–33 ft) long, it was much, much bigger. Its body was protected by bony plates, and it had a heavy club of bone at the end of its tail. When angry or in danger, *Ankylosaurus* turned its head away from its enemy (for protection) and walloped hard with its tail club.

Large tail clubs were supported by a rod-like section of tail. This enabled the dinosaur to swing it with great force.

FIGHTING BEASTS

Ankylosaurus could break the bones of any predator that came too close. But despite its tail club, it remained vulnerable. If a *Tyrannosaurus* saw an *Ankylosaurus* grazing, it would try to flip the heavy beast over and bite its softer underbelly.

SNAPPING JAWS

Dinosaurs were not the only monsters to roam the planet in prehistoric times. Huge creatures with snapping jaws lurked in the swamps, swam in the oceans and swooped and screeched in the skies overhead.

11A ▶

11A ▶   12

PREDATOR X

A huge, fossilized sea monster, known as "Predator X" (*Pliosaurus funkei*), was found in 2006 in Svalbard, in the Arctic Ocean. Scientists estimate that it measured up to 12.8 m (42 ft) long, and had a bite four times more powerful than *Tyrannosaurus*! They have described it as "the most fearsome animal ever to swim in the oceans."

ARCHAEOPTERYX

A fossilized reptile named *Archaeopteryx* (say are-kee-OP-ter-ix), first found in 1861, had feathers and primitive wings. Experts think it did not fly like a true bird, but probably glided from trees or rocks to escape being caught by a hungry predator.

REAL LIFE DRAGONS!

Pterosaurs were more like dragons than birds. Some, such as *Pterodactylus* (shown here), were not much bigger than a seagull, but the giant *Quetzalcoatlus* was as big as a light airplane. Pterosaurs glided on bat-like wings of skin stretched between their long, bony fingers. Unlike some dinosaurs, pterosaurs had scales, not feathers.

Plesiosaurs were long-necked ocean-dwellers that preyed on fish, molluscs and other marine animals. Some people believe that Scotland's legendary Loch Ness Monster may in fact be a long-lost plesiosaur!

SWAMP MONSTER

The prehistoric crocodile *Sarcosuchus* was a lumbering giant about twice as long and ten times as heavy as a crocodile today. It lurked in rivers and swamps where dinosaurs came to drink, and would lunge at them with its huge jaws if they came too close. Any unwary dinosaur would quickly be snapped up for lunch!

AMAZING!

KRONOSAURUS

At 9–10 m (30–33 ft) long, *Kronosaurus* was one of the largest pliosaurs. Its huge jaws were filled with numerous teeth, the longest measuring up to 30 cm (12 in.) long. Although not serrated, its teeth were capable of trapping turtles and plesiosaurs, and it may also have fed on giant squid.

17

BEASTLY CREATURES

The natural world can be a savage place, where creatures need to be mean to stay alive – they kill to eat, or kill to avoid being eaten. Some animals only reveal their mean streak when they have to save the lives of their young, while others find that being foul just comes easily to them.

DID YOU KNOW?

MICRO-BEASTS

In the wild world of deadly animals, there are more tiny terrors than bloodthirsty giants. Some of them are so small that they actually live inside other creatures (the hosts), and change the way those animals behave. Some burrow into their flesh, some cause nasty infections, and one even eats a fish's tongue and then becomes the new tongue itself – yuck!

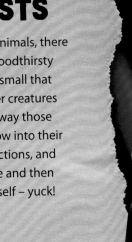

COOL KILLERS

Some of the nasty surprises that animals have in store to keep attackers away include toxic skin, venomous fangs, super-sticky slime and loads of tiny, sharp teeth. Spiders are supremely savage and have a collection of cool killer skills. They can find, catch, chase or trap their prey, and then stab them with fangs that deliver a nasty dose of venom. Some types of spider can even shoot horrid, itchy hairs at an attacker!

WATCH OUT!

Nowhere is safe. Animals manage to survive in almost every part of the world, from the deepest oceans to icy mountain-tops. A quick dip in a river might alert a toothy piranha fish, while a walk in the jungle might get the attention of a monster-sized lizard. Most beastly animals, from slithering snakes to crouching tigers, like to surprise their prey.

Wild pigs are meaner – and smarter – than they look. They are fearless woodland animals that charge headfirst at anyone, or anything, that comes too close.

SMELLIEST ANIMALS

Some animals can produce a really bad smell, especially if they feel threatened. Best keep clear of these animals if you don't want to stink, too!

OLD MUSK

The musk ox has been causing a stink since the time of the mammoths. It has lived in North America for up to 200,000 years. Although it looks like a small American bison, it is more closely related to sheep. The musk ox gets its name from the strong smell of musk in its wee that it sprays on itself and on the ground during the breeding season. Although we think the smell is terrible, female musk oxen are attracted by it!

HOW COOL!

TENTACLES

A slug may not smell too bad itself, but it has four nose-like tentacles for detecting smells, so it better not get too close to these stinky animals!

SPRAY ALERT!

The bombardier beetle is known for the foul, boiling chemicals that it shoots out of its rear. Allegedly, legendary naturalist Charles Darwin popped one in his mouth to free up a hand during a beetle-collecting expedition, and experienced the stink (and probably taste!) of the beetle's spray.

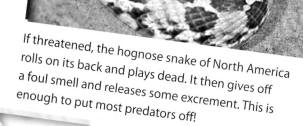

If threatened, the hognose snake of North America rolls on its back and plays dead. It then gives off a foul smell and releases some excrement. This is enough to put most predators off!

AMAZING FACT!

ULTIMATE STINKER

The skunk is the most famous stinker in the world. It has stink glands in its bottom that it uses to spray a really disgusting liquid at any attacker. The liquid, which can be smelled by humans up to 1 mile (1.6 km) away, can irritate the skin of the attacker and even blind them for a time. One creature that will prey on skunks is the great horned owl, which has no sense of smell!

DID YOU KNOW?

NATIVE PERFUME

The striped polecat is a skunk-like member of the weasel family. Its anal glands can allegedly be smelled from 0.5 mile (0.8 km) away. While the animal's smell is amazing enough, even more amazing is the fact that some native peoples actually use the polecat's incredibly nasty secretions as a perfume!

21

SKIN SHEDDERS

Imagine if your skin was too small for you! Some animals' bodies grow, but their skin stays the same size, so they have to shed their old skin and grow a new, bigger one.

Shed skin can make a healthy snack for a lizard as it contains valuable minerals, such as calcium. This is why lizards often nibble at their own skin when it starts to shed.

REVOLTING MOLTING

Most lizards shed their skin in patches, but when a snake slithers out of its skin it leaves behind one whole piece (like this rattlesnake skin). Losing all the skin in one go is called molting. Animals usually stop eating for at least a few days to prepare for a molt.

WATCH OUT!

DEADLY RATTLE

The rattles at the end of a rattlesnake's tail are made up of layers of shed, dry skin that make a noise when shaken. The noise warns other animals to keep clear of the snake and its deadly bite.

SKINNED

Snakeskins are often used to make handbags (purses), wallets and shoes. Molted skin is too thin to be used, so snakes are kept in farms where first they are starved, so their skins loosen, and then they are pumped with water so the skins stretch. Finally they are killed.

PLAYING DEAD

Spiders don't have a bony skeleton like us – instead they have a really strong skin, called an exoskeleton. The exoskeleton doesn't grow, so when a spider gets bigger its old skin cracks open, and the new, soft-skinned spider steps out. If you spot a tarantula lying on its back, beware! Although it may look dead, it might actually just be molting.

When a young insect – such as a cicada – turns into an adult, it goes through a big body change called a metamorphosis. The old skin splits open and the adult simply climbs out!

DID YOU KNOW?

SLITHER AND SLIDE

Baby garter snakes get a new skin within minutes of being born. The molt can take less than five minutes once it has started. The paper-thin old skin is left behind as the snake slides away – it's like pulling a leg out of a long sock!

ANIMAL SLIME

What's the point of slime? It may look and feel disgusting, but slime is very useful. Without it, some animals simply couldn't survive.

GOO IS GOOD!

Slime helps snails and slugs to slither along the ground, over stones and prickles and up walls. Slime is so tough that a slug can even glide along a razor blade without getting hurt! Slugs dry out very easily, but a thick coat of slime helps them to stay moist. Snails have hard shells, so they don't dry out as easily as slugs, but they still need slime to help them slide.

MEAT-EATER

Most slugs are happy to eat vegetables and other plants, but some giant slugs, such as Spanish slugs, also graze on dead animals. When groups of them feed on roadkill, their slime is slimy enough to send cars sideways!

SNAIL TREATS

Snail slime has been used to make spot creams and to treat wounds, and snail eggs are appearing on menus in some restaurants. People say they are a bit like caviar, but have a more "earthy" taste!

MEGA-SLIME

You know you've got giant African land snails living in your garden because they leave huge slime trails and long, ribbon-like poops! Each snail grows to 20 cm (8 in.) long, and eats flowers, vegetables and fruit. Little worms live inside these snails – a single snail may have thousands of worms wriggling away inside it. In some places, the snails are considered a real treat, and are eaten raw.

Hagfish don't have spines and they don't even have jaws, but they do have super-strong, super-stretchy slime. Their skin makes mucus packed with lots of threads. When the mucus combines with water, it expands in size and stickiness, making it almost impossible for sharks to bite the fish.

DID YOU KNOW?

USEFUL?

To scrape off old slime, a hagfish ties itself in a knot, then slides the knot down its body. Scientists hope to use the hagfish's slime recipe to make clothes and even bulletproof vests.

25

VENOMOUS FANGS

Venom is a type of poison that is injected into a victim's body. A set of sharp fangs is the perfect way to deliver a deadly dose of venom.

DEADLY BITE

Rattlesnakes have amazing fangs that fold up into their mouths when they are not needed. The fangs are hollow, and when the snake bites it can choose to send venom down through the fangs and into its victim's flesh. If there is no venom, the bite is "dry" and the victim escapes with a warning!

DID YOU KNOW?

MILKING VENOM

Scientists are able to milk the venom from a snake by carefully squeezing it out of the snake's venom glands into a dish. The venom is then used to make antivenin (or antivenom), which is used to treat snakebites. The antivenin neutralizes the venom and prevents it causing further damage, but it cannot undo any damage already done. For this reason it is very important that it is administered as soon as possible after the bite.

Tarantulas are scary-looking spiders. They can grow to the size of a dinner plate, and have heavy bodies with long, hairy legs. Their 2.5 cm (1 in.) long fangs can inject venom that attacks nerve cells, causing terrible pain.

Instructions on page 5

SCAN ME

SUPER SPITTER

Spitting cobras can fire a jet of nasty venom at an attacker, and are accurate in their aim most of the time. Even when the attacker is moving, a cobra can still hit its target – usually in the eyes. The venom causes intense pain, or even blindness.

DYING FOR LOVE

Black widow spiders are some of the most feared of all spiders. It is almost impossible to feel the spider bite, but its venom moves quickly into the victim's body, attacking the nerves, making the heart beat too fast or too slow, and causing sweating and pain. Female black widows sometimes kill and eat their own mates, which is why they are called "widows."

SUPER FACT!

ON THE PROWL

Funnel web spiders like to hide in dark places until it is mating time. Then they get really brave! Males dart around searching for females, and they won't let anything get in their way. When a male Sydney funnel web spider is scared, it rears up on its back legs and prepares to leap forward and bite, often biting over and over again. In 2010, a swarm of deadly Sydney funnel web spiders caused havoc in the Australian city. Parents were warned to keep their children safe, as they are more likely to die from a spider bite than adults.

WATCH OUT!

SNAKE ALERT!

Taipans have one of the deadliest venoms of all snakes, but Indian cobras kill far more people – 10,000 a year in India alone – because they live alongside humans.

27

SERIOUSLY CREEPY WEBS

Spider silk is tougher than rubber or bone, and it is half as strong as steel. It's the perfect material for building creepy webs and traps.

While some spiders build beautifully neat webs, others spin their silk into messy cobwebs. Daddy longleg spiders build the messiest webs of all. They hide inside their web and wait for other spiders to walk by – then they pounce.

WORLD'S WIDEST WEB

The biggest orb webs in the world are made by Darwin's bark spider, from the African island of Madagascar. The webs can cover an area up to 2.8 sq m (30 sq ft). You wouldn't want to stumble into one of those in the dark!

STRETCHY SILK

Spiders produce silk in their spigot, and use their legs to pull the threads out to build a web. The silk is covered with glue that sticks to victims, and it's also very stretchy – it can stretch six times its length before snapping.

GOLDEN ORB

Animals that walk or fly into a web quickly find themselves stuck to it and unable to escape. Golden orb web spiders can build webs that are big enough to trap bats and birds. One large specimen even tried to eat a brown tree snake that got caught in its web.

TOUGHEST WEB

Darwin's bark spider not only builds the biggest orb webs. It also breaks the record for spinning the toughest silk in the world. Its silk is twice as tough as any other spider silk known, and ten times tougher than the synthetic material called Kevlar, which is used to make cables and brake linings.

COOL FACT!

AMAZINGLY STRONG

One thread of spider silk is made up of lots of thinner threads. These vary in thickness from 0.003 to 0.008 mm (0.00012 to 0.00032 in.) across. If a fibre of silk could be made 20 mm (0.8 in.) thick, it would be strong enough to lift a truck!

DUNG LOVERS

Dung, poo, poop or feces – we have lots of names for waste, but for some animals it's a tasty dish on the menu!

SCARY DUNG

Gardeners have discovered that putting lion dung near their growing vegetables stops local cats from digging them up. As cats are territorial, even the bravest of them will back off quickly if they can smell that a lion has been there first. The lion dung is also good for fertilizing the vegetables!

BUG ALERT!

Did you know that up to one-third of the weight of your pillow could be made up of dust mites, dust mite poo and dead skin? While you are sleeping, the dust mites inside your pillow are busily munching on little flakes of your dead skin. Enzymes in their feces often make people wheeze. Have a good night!

STINKY BREAKFAST

Mountain gorillas like nothing more than a hot, steaming breakfast of... their own dung! Lots of animals eat their own poop from time to time, including rabbits, wolves, chimps and dogs.

Some dung beetles bury themselves inside a ball of dung and make a happy home inside. Some lay their eggs inside dung, while others turn a pile of dung into a delicious meal. The beetles roll their balls of dung to a safe place to use later.

FACT FILE

Ring-tailed lemurs like eating each other's dung.

Terrible hairy flies live in caves in Africa and feed on bat poop.

Wombat poop is cube-shaped.

Turkey vultures poo on their own feet to cool them down. The poop also kills the bacteria that would thrive on their blood-soaked talons.

A single blue whale poop can be bigger than a human!

Treehoppers are bizarre bugs that prefer to stay hidden from view so no one eats them. Some of them look like bird poop – that's a great disguise!

Yellow dung flies attack the bugs that feed on steaming piles of sloppy cow dung! They also lay their eggs on the dung.

DEAD FLESH EATERS

Scavengers are happy to eat whatever stinky carrion (dead animals) they find lying around.

AMAZING!

FAST EATERS

In hot weather, flies and their maggots could eat more than half of a human body in just one week.

DID YOU KNOW?

MAGGOTS

Maggots spend their time feeding and growing. They can increase in length by ten times in just four days. Using the little hooks around their mouths, they scrape at flesh. They have breathing holes in their bottoms, which means they can get properly stuck into their food and still breathe!

Hyenas will chomp through almost anything. They especially like to gorge on carrion, and they make light work of crushing bones in their mighty jaws.

CARRION CROW

Carrion crows are smart birds that can eat almost anything. They eat dead animals, but also attack nests and kill chicks.

BAD BREATH BEARS!

Some bears like to eat fish – dead or alive. They have been known to follow ravens in order to find dead fish to eat.

FLESH-FACED FEASTING

Why do vultures have bald faces? It's so they don't end up with blood-soaked feathers! When these big birds tuck in for a gruesome feeding frenzy, they end up covered in blood and gore. Since bacteria feed on blood and dead flesh, they could suffer from nasty skin infections. A featherless face is much easier to keep clean.

Sexton beetles dig holes under a dead animal so it falls in to a pit. Then they bury it, and the female lays her eggs nearby. When the young hatch, their parents feed them meat from the dead body.

FOUL FLIES

Long ago, people thought that dead animals turned into flies, because they noticed that maggots – which are young flies – live in meat. In fact, flies and other bugs lay their eggs in carrion because it is a great food for their young. A female fly lays up to 300 eggs at a time, and they hatch in just one day – yuck!

11A
12
11A
12

33

BLOOD SUCKERS

Drinking blood may seem disgusting, but it is an almost perfect food. It contains sugar for energy, water, iron and muscle-building protein.

DID YOU KNOW?

NIGHT CREEPERS

Is it true that vampire bats feed on humans? Yes it is! They are more likely to feed on the blood of cows and horses, but vampire bats also sneak up on sleeping people and sink their razor-sharp fangs into ankles and feet.

WORLD'S DEADLIEST INSECT

Female mosquitoes need a blood meal before they lay their eggs. While they are sucking human blood, they can pass malaria – a killer disease – on to the person whose blood they are sucking.

BIG FEEDERS

Leeches are soft, squidgy, slimy blood-suckers. They slice through skin using three blade-like jaws and suck up the blood that pours out. Leeches can drink five times their own bodyweight in blood. They can also store lots of blood in their bodies – some of them only need to feed twice a year!

TERRIBLE TICKS

This nasty-looking bug is a member of the spider family, and it has a taste for blood. Ticks bury their jaws into a victim's flesh and suck out the blood with a straw-like mouthpart. While they feed, ticks can pass deadly diseases to their victims.

COOL FACT!

SNEAKY

Animals that drink blood are called hematophages (say heem-at-oh-fay-jes). Many blood-feeders are able to stop the blood from clotting, so it keeps flowing. They also pour painkillers into their victims, so they can't feel their skin being broken.

JUMP FOR JOY

Fleas scurry around on a victim's skin, hiding between strands of hair. They pierce the skin and suck up the blood that pools there. Once they have fed, fleas drop off their victims' bodies and snooze in their beds or nests instead. When it's time for tea, a flea can jump back on to its host using its super-springy legs – it can leap 200 times its own body length!

PESKY PARASITES

Meet the nastiest, most disgusting animals on the planet. These creepy creatures have such gruesome lifestyles you may never feel the same way about wildlife again!

DID YOU KNOW?

UNWELCOME VISITORS

Animals that live on, or inside, another animal are called parasites. They get their food from the other animal, which is called the "host." Over time, the parasite makes the host ill, or even kills it.

BOT FLIES

Adult bot flies drop their larvae on to the skin of an animal, such as a horse, or a human. The larvae burrow into the host's flesh, feeding on it and causing nasty wounds and infections that weep and ooze all the time. In horses, the larvae eventually pass out in the animal's dung. Adult bot flies emerge from the dung 2 to 8 weeks later.

MINI MONSTERS

Many parasites are too small to see, but they can still be deadly. Toxoplasmas are tiny creatures that live in rats, mice, cats and people. When they are inside rats, these pests make their hosts fearless, and especially keen on cats – they love the smell of cat wee! As the rats get closer to the cats, the cats are able to catch and eat them, and they become infected, too.

EXPLODING FLY

If you find a splattered fly, it may be the victim of a type of fungus that grew inside the fly's body, dissolving all of its body bits from the inside out! When it's ready, the fungus makes the fly explode and splatter.

LIVER FLUKE

Liver fluke worms lay eggs that hatch in water. The young swim about until they find a water snail, which they burrow into. When they are ready, the young flukes burst out of the snail's flesh and settle down on some juicy green grass, waiting for a sheep or cow to come and feed. Once inside their new host (the sheep or cow), the liver flukes feed on blood in the animal's liver, and their eggs are passed out in its poop.

AMAZING!

LUNGWORMS

Lungworms like to settle down inside an animal's lungs, where they cause terrible harm. Dogs can become infected if they drink water or eat slugs (often lurking inside apples) infected with lungworm larvae.

STRANGE ANTICS

Young lancet liver flukes live first inside snails, and then inside ants. Once inside the ants, they change the ants' behavior, making them want to climb to the tops of grass stems. There they get eaten by cows, and the flukes have successfully gained a new host.

37

FAMOUS MAN-EATERS!

It's a violent, vicious world out there, and sometimes animals and humans become deadly enemies when beasts turn into man-eaters.

TOP TIP!

STAND TALL

American alligators have killed at least 400 people in the state of Florida since 1948. Should you ever find yourself confronted by an alligator, stand as tall as you can! Alligators are more likely to attack people who are sitting, swimming or lying down.

TWO-TOED TOM

Two-toed Tom was a huge, man-eating alligator. He was described as a "red-eyed hell demon" and he terrified people who lived near his swampy home in Alabama, USA. Tom soon gained a scary reputation for killing cows, mules and people – but he was never caught! For many years, all hunters saw of him were his two-toed footprints on the muddy riverbanks.

TERRIBLE TIGER

The most famous man-eater of all time was the Champawat tiger. She is listed in the Guinness Book of World Records as the most successful animal killer of humans ever known. Totally fearless, she would calmly approach anyone she saw and grab them in her jaws. She killed at least 426 people in India and Nepal, and it took a team of more than 300 men to eventually find and kill her, in 1907.

More than 50 years ago a sloth bear in Mysore, India, became a man-eater, killing at least 12 people. It always attacked the face of its victim, clawing and biting its prey to death.

WATCH OUT!

ON THE PROWL

Hyenas have almost no fear of humans. Spotted hyenas will sneak into tents to grab a mouthful of human flesh before running off to chew it in peace. The ones that turn man-eater tend to be very large – a pair responsible for killing 27 people in Malawi in 1962 weighed 72 kg (159 lb) and 77 kg (170 lb).

HUNGRY AS A LION

Lions don't normally attack people, but when they are hungry they stop being too fussy! Between 1932 and 1947, a pride of lions in Tanzania, Africa, got a taste for human flesh when they couldn't find any other food. They stalked the local villagers, and managed to devour at least 1,500 people before they were eventually shot.

SCAN ME
Instructions on page 5

MORE TERRIBLE TEETH

Teeth can stab, crunch, slice, tear, grind, grip, rip and chew. Animals with teeth have got a great set of weapons, and they can do some gruesome damage.

FOUL FISH

There are stories of piranhas killing humans and stripping their flesh to the bones in minutes, although they are actually much more likely to attack smaller prey. They often attack as a group. With their razor-sharp teeth they can easily slice off a mouthful of flesh!

TIGER TREATS

Tigers need gigantic jaws and impressive teeth to turn a grazing animal into lunch. They use their large fangs, up to 10 cm (4 in.) long, to stab their prey, and scissor-like teeth to slice flesh. Strong molars are perfect for crunching bones up into tasty mouthfuls that are easy to swallow. Yum!

CANNY CANINES

Those mighty teeth look like deadly daggers, but baboons are just big show-offs. When two male baboons are thinking about having a fight, they each do a big yawn to see who's got the biggest fangs. Usually, one male will get the hint and run away!

MONSTER OF THE DEEP SEA

Down in the deep, dark parts of the ocean there are some ugly animals! Deep sea anglerfish look creepy and have a sneaky way of catching their prey. Above the fish's head is a long spine, tipped with a special light that tempts other fish to come close. In the darkness, a victim can't see the enormous, toothy mouth behind the light… until it's too late!

DID YOU KNOW?

ANGRY ANTS

Trap-jawed ants – up to a million of these ants live together in treetops. They attack prey 100 times bigger than themselves and rip flesh with their powerful jaws.

Fire ants – when a fire ant bites, it holds tight with its jaws so it can pump in plenty of venom, which causes unbearable pain.

Army ants – when a group of these ants is on the move, it's best to run fast! They swarm over everything in their path, biting, stinging and munching as they go.

CROC ATTACKS!

Crocs are fearless killing machines that lurk in rivers and lakes waiting for lunch to come by. They attack with super speed and strength.

LYING IN WAIT

When crocodiles are snoozing in the water, they look slow and harmless, but they can swing into action in a flash. Often they creep up on their victims – they have even been known to sneak into campers' tents for a human-sized snack. In Africa, Nile crocodiles eat about 1,000 people a year.

BLOODBATH

During the Second World War, 1,000 Japanese soldiers were escaping at night through a swamp on Ramree Island, off the coast of Burma (now Myanmar). Their screams could be heard far away by the Allies as saltwater crocodiles moved in for the attack – many of the soldiers never made it out of the swamp alive.

KILLER CROC

Gustave is a killer-croc celebrity that has featured in wildlife films and books. He lives in Burundi, Africa, and at 6 m (20 ft) long, is probably the largest predator in the whole of Africa. It is rumored that Gustave has killed more than 300 people, but it's likely that he's had some help from his croc friends. No one knows if he is still alive, but if he is, Gustave is now more than 50 years old.

TERRIBLE TEETH

Crocodile jaws are huge and lined with teeth, and their bodies are packed with mighty muscles. A big crocodile can bite a person's head off with a single snap of its jaws! Once a crocodile has got its victim in its jaws, it often dives underwater, rolling around to drown its victim and crush its bones.

SNACK ATTACK

In 2007, a sleeping saltwater crocodile in a Taiwan zoo was being examined by a vet. Unfortunately it woke up and bit the vet's arm clean off. Luckily the arm was rescued from the croc's jaws just in time, and doctors were able to stitch it back on.

GREAT WHITE DANGER

Just one bone-crunching bite from a great white shark can be deadly. These massive hunters rule the seas, filling people's hearts with fear.

FISH OF FEAR

Great white sharks are ruthless, intelligent hunters with amazing senses – they can detect a single drop of blood in the water around them. The sharks plan their attacks, and swim with power and speed.

NO ESCAPE!

Great whites have 50 to 60 large teeth in each jaw. The teeth are saw-like and super-sharp. Once a great white has its victim in its jaws, it shakes its head from side to side, so its teeth can slice and saw their way through bone.

FACT FILE

Great whites grow to about 5.2 m (17 ft) long, but bigger ones have been spotted!

Humans kill as many as 100 million sharks every year.

You are twenty times more likely to be killed by a dog than by a shark, and forty times more likely to be struck by lightning.

EYES ON THE PRIZE

When a great white has spotted a seal, it sneaks up from behind, swimming silently toward its victim. As it gets closer, it turns on the speed. Attacking from below, it slams its jaws into the flesh of the seal and bites off a big chunk.

COOL FACT!

TEETH

Sharks have several rows of teeth in each jaw. When teeth in the front row get blunt or break, they are quickly replaced by new teeth from the row behind.

SINK OR SWIM?

It's not much of a choice, but if you had to choose to be attacked by an alligator or a shark, you should choose the shark – you would be twice as likely to survive!

Shark Attacks
Red = high for the area, blue = average, green = low.
Orange (USA only) is midway between blue and red.

VICTIMS

There have been about 300 unprovoked attacks on humans by great whites in the last 500 years. About one-third of the victims died. Generally, after just one bite of a human, great whites swim off in disgust – they seem to think that people taste gross!

STINGERS

A wicked sting can cause mind-boggling pain. Not all stings are deadly, but some are so agonizing that they make the victim wish they were dead.

Deathstalkers are some of the most dangerous scorpions on the planet. They use their pincers to grab prey, and the sharp stinger on their tail to inject deadly venom. When scared, they attack humans to defend themselves.

11A ▶   12

12

STINGERS

RINGS OF DEATH

The blue-ringed octopus is a pretty little animal that could fit on the palm of your hand, but beware its nasty bite! It can deliver venom that is strong enough to kill a person, making this the deadliest octopus in the seas.

SEA WASPS

Jellyfish tentacles are covered in tiny, stinging harpoons that fire out, stab a victim and inject a nasty dose of venom. One of the most dangerous jellyfish in the oceans is the box jellyfish (also known as a stinger or sea wasp in Australia). If you swim through the almost invisible tentacles of a box jellyfish, you can expect searing pain and toxins that affect your heart, skin cells and nervous system. The pain is so bad that it can make your heart stop!

OUCH!

Most starfish are harmless – they have five arms and blunt spines on their bodies – but crown of thorns starfish can have up to 21 arms and they are covered in venomous spines. They also have disgusting table manners! They empty their stomachs onto the tiny animals that live in coral, and the burning juices turn them into soupy, gloopy liquid that the starfish then eats.

WATCH OUT!

DEATH SQUADS

Groups of 30 Asian giant hornets gang up to attack honeybee hives, bringing death and destruction. They rip the heads off the bees and move in to the hive so they can feast on honey and bee grubs.

DANGER!

The Asian giant hornet is a particularly gruesome insect. At 5 cm (2 in.) long, it's the length of a person's thumb! Imagine the pain that its 6 mm (0.2 in.) stinger can inflict – it's been described as "a hot nail." An injection of adrenalin is used to treat people who have been stung. It stops their body going into shock, which can be fatal.

47

CUNNING KILLERS

These scary animals have got some stomach-churning hunting tricks. They need to be cunning killers to get food in their bellies, and stay alive.

Jumping spiders spot a victim, move into position and leap – sometimes more than 20 times their own body length – onto their prey.

Dinosaurs disappeared long ago, but Komodo dragons are a reminder of how they lived. These giant lizards are ruthless meat-eaters with a nasty bite and venom in their spit. Komodos get together in hunting packs to chase animals and people. If peckish, they even turn cannibal and eat their own young.

DID YOU KNOW?

SLOW LORIS

A slow loris might look cute and cuddly, with its big eyes and innocent face, but watch out! This animal is cunning – it makes poison, which it mixes with spit to make a paste. Lorises keep some of the paste in their mouths, in case they need to bite an attacker, and they spread some of it on their fur. Any animal that gets a mouthful suffers terrible stomach pains.

BIG SQUEEZE!

Constrictor snakes squeeze the life out of an animal and then swallow it whole! A boa constrictor will grab its prey and wrap its mighty coils around the creature's body. Every time the victim breathes out, the snake squeezes a little tighter. Eventually, the poor creature dies from crushed bones and suffocation, and is swallowed.

AMAZING!

FROG ALERT!

Many little forest frogs look harmless, but have skin that is coated with a poison that kills in seconds. A red-eyed tree-frog may not have toxic skin, but it has looks that kill! Its big, red eyes almost pop out of its head, and it flashes its big orange feet. It's so scary that most attackers run away!

TOP DOG

African hunting dogs are cunning killers that use their pack power to attack large prey, such as antelopes. They don't waste time sneaking up on a victim – hunting dogs work together to chase their target, snapping at its heels and grabbing mouthfuls of flesh. Eventually the victim collapses, too exhausted to run or fight back.

UGLY ALERT!

Beauty is in the eye of the beholder. Some people think these creatures are freaky and gross, others think they are gorgeous!

NUDE DUDES

Skinny, scrawny, wrinkled and repulsive to look at, naked mole rats live in warm, underground burrows, so they don't need fur. These sabre-toothed sausages use their long teeth to dig and slice through roots. They live in big groups ruled by a single female, the queen, who stops the other females from having babies.

CHILLY CAT

Sphynx cats have so little fur they often need to wear specially made clothes to keep warm! Their skin is velvety smooth to touch, and is the color their fur would be if they had any. Hairless cats can easily get sunburned and dirty, so they need a weekly bath!

11A ▶ 12

11A ▶ 12

BALDY

When baby rats and mice are born, they are almost completely hairless. Sometimes the fur they need to keep them warm simply never grows, and they also lack the whiskers they need to help them find their way in the dark.

BLOBFISH

Deep in the ocean around Australia lives what looks like a ball of slime with a miserable mouth. In fact it's a blobfish! This fish lives at depths between 600 to 1,200 m (2,000 to 4,000 ft), where the pressure is too intense for normal fish with fins and muscles to swim. The blobfish's gooey, jelly-like appearance allows it to float just above the ocean floor, swallowing any food that floats by.

When a male proboscis monkey jumps through the trees, its long nose wobbles about and sometimes flips up and hits the monkey in the face!

SMOOTH POOCHES

Most dogs have a thick coat of fur to keep them warm, but some dogs have been bred without much hair. They might have a thin coat of fur, or tufts of hair on their heads, legs and tails. Ancient Native American tribes kept hairless dogs to warm up their beds, and sometimes they ate them, too!

51

BIRDS WITH ATTITUDE

Some birds sing pretty songs and peck at worms, but others are more violent. These feathered fiends are killers with attitude.

BIG KICKERS

Cassowaries are the third-largest birds in the world. They can't fly, but they are so fast and strong that they can disembowel a victim with one quick kick. Does this remind you of dinosaur behavior? Scientists think that the deep, booming call of a cassowary may be similar to the noises made by dinosaurs, too.

Cassowaries have a claw on each foot that grows to 10 cm (4 in.) long, and can be used to stab an attacker.

AMAZING!

STAMPER

Secretary birds have the longest legs of any bird of prey, and they put them to good use. Although they can fly, they prefer to walk, often up to 20 miles (32 km) a day, stalking rats, mice and snakes, which they kick or stamp to death.

52

TOXIC BIRDS

Only one type of venomous bird has ever been discovered – the hooded pitohui of Papua New Guinea. The feathers contain a nasty poison that causes pain and irritation if touched. Pitohuis have an amazing way of making the poison. They get it from toxic beetles that they eat. The birds are unaffected by the poison, and store it in their bodies.

The great horned owl is said to have a grip (with its claws) equal to the bite of an adult German shepherd dog.

SILENT SWOOP

Great horned owls swoop silently down to catch prey, grasping the victim in their giant talons (claws). They eat mice and rats whole, but prefer to strip birds of their feathers, legs and wingtips before tucking in. With a wingspan of up to 152 cm (60 in.), they are big enough to attack cats, dogs, turkeys and even young alligators. They have also attacked people who have got too close to their nests.

More Fearsome Flyers

Watch out – there are birds about! Some birds can swoop, dive and attack with a deadly force.

FULL OF NOISE

Herring gulls are large, noisy birds that eat almost anything they can find, including chicks that they find in other birds' nests. Gulls feast on garbage tips, but they are fearless, and are just as happy to grab food out of people's hands. They dive-bomb picnickers and people in their gardens, squawking as they swoop. Their large bills are strong enough to cause nasty injuries.

RUN!

The American bald eagle has a wingspan of about 2 m (6 ft). It is strong enough to swoop down and grab a mule deer, weighing 7 kg (14 lb), in its mighty talons and carry it off.

GONE

Some of the largest eagles that ever lived were Haast's eagles, with an incredible 3 m (10 ft) wingspan. They lived in New Zealand until people turned up and ate them all.

FLYING PIRATES

Skuas are big bullies – other seabirds try to keep as far away from them as possible. When a skua is hungry, it doesn't bother to catch its own food, but instead steals it from other birds. Its favorite trick is to fly up to a bird that has a fish in its beak and grab it by its wing, so it can't fly and falls to the ground. The skua then chases after it, pecking viciously until it gives up its fish.

AMAZING!

BUTCHERS

Butcher birds deserve their nasty name – they catch bugs and impale them on sharp thorns or twigs. The bugs can wriggle, but they can't escape, so the bird can eat them more easily. Sometimes the birds leave the bugs for a while, returning later to eat them when they are hungry.

ANGRY BIRDS

Arctic terns are often called sea swallows, but "angry birds" would be a better name! Parent birds don't like anyone to get close to their nests, and they'll attack anyone who does. They aim their strong, red beaks at the back of a person's head – and often draw blood.

MONSTERS OF THE DEEP

The deepest part of the ocean is cold and dark, and the weight of water pressing down can crush a body to pulp!

EIGHT-ARMED MEAT EATER

Giant octopuses can grow up to 5 m (16 ft) long. These mega-marine monsters have four pairs of arms, and each of these is covered with up to 280 suckers. The octopuses seek out their prey of fish, crabs, lobsters and other octopuses, and grab them with their strong arms.

Giant squid distribution

SCARY SQUID

The first giant squid was discovered by sailors in 1639. Stories of this massive ocean beast quickly spread. People feared the creatures would attack their boats and sink them. Female giant squids are bigger than males and can grow to 15 m (50 ft) long – that's as long as a bus. They have long tentacles that can grip hold of wriggly prey, such as fish and jellyfish, but thankfully they don't attack boats.

YUCK!

Octopuses have some gross eating habits! They use a special tooth-covered body part to drill a hole through a victim's shell. Then they pour in a poison that dissolves the flesh that glues the animal to its shell.

FREAKY FOUL FISH

A sea lamprey has lots of pointed teeth and a sucking mouth. This foul fish attaches its mouth to the side of a fish and then starts to scrape away at its victim's flesh with its rasping teeth. As blood and bits of flesh ooze, the lamprey laps it all up.

COOL FACT!

MARINE SNOW

Billions of bits of dead animal skin and flesh, dead plants and animal poop fall gently to the bottom of the ocean and make a mega-deep slush, called ooze!

WELL, WELL, WHALE!

What are the biggest animals in the world, with the biggest bellies and biggest poops? Whales, of course!

IN DANGER

It is thought that about 350,000 blue whales were killed in the last century. There are probably fewer than 5,000 alive today. Hunting is banned in international waters, but deep-sea fishing, heavy sea traffic and the whales' slow rate of reproduction keep their number low.

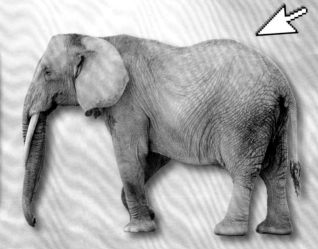

GENTLE GIANT

Blue whales are the largest animals that have ever lived. These massive beasts eat animals called krill that are smaller than your hand. One adult blue whale can eat up to 3,600 kg (7,900 lb) of krill a day. The krill are pink, which explains why blue whales have pink poop! A single poop can be 3 m (10 ft) long!

THIRSTY WORK

Whales are mammals, like us. That means they feed their babies with milk – and lots of it! Baby southern right whales can drink up to 200 litres (422 pints) of milk a day.

HUGE TONGUES

A blue whale's tongue is about the size and weight of a full-grown African elephant. It weighs about 2.7 tonnes (3 tons) – roughly the same as 2,700 bags of sugar!

STINKY STUFF!

Foul-smelling stuff called ambergris is made in the guts of sperm whales. It is passed out with their poop, and believe it or not is very valuable because it can be turned into a sweet-smelling perfume!

BLUBBER AND BONES

Whales have a thick layer of fat, called blubber, that keeps the whale warm in cold water. In the past, blubber was minced into chunks and boiled on board whaling ships, to produce oil for machinery and burning in lamps. Whales also store oil in their bones, which are softer than the bones of land mammals.

BIG IS BEST

The largest blue whale ever measured was 33.5 m (100 ft) long and its heart was the size of a small car. The blood vessels of blue whales are so big that a human can crawl through them. The babies are huge, too – a blue whale baby weighs the same as nearly 900 human babies!

CREEPY CRUSTACEANS

Crabs, lobsters and krill are just a few of the ocean's creepy crustaceans.

LET'S BOOGIE!

Smelly boy blue crabs like to boogie! They wave their pincers about to make their smell travel farther. Females like the smell, and come scuttling over to make friends.

TONGUE- EATING LOUSE

The tongue-eating louse has a particularly revolting habit. After it has finished eating a fish's tongue, it attaches itself to the stub of the tongue and becomes the fish's new tongue. Some tongue-eating lice feed on the host fish's blood and others feed on fish mucus.

Coconut crabs are enormous, measuring up to 1 m (39 in.) from leg tip to leg tip. They climb palm trees and use their enormous claws to get at the soft flesh inside a coconut.

CRABZILLA

Japanese spider crabs are 3.8 m (12 ft) across from one claw tip to another – that makes them the biggest crustaceans on Earth (and much bigger than a diver!). Their bodies stay the same size as they age, but their legs get longer and weaker.

LEFT HOOK

Most crabs use their claws to frighten other animals, but boxer crabs keep stinging anemones on their claws and wave them about like boxing gloves! The crabs look scary, so other animals stay away. The anemones don't mind because they eat food left over from the crab's meals!

GIANT ISOPOD

This beast is the massive cousin of the pillbug (woodlouse). Unlike woodlice, however, giant isopods feast on dead whales instead of rotting plants, so perhaps it's no surprise they can grow so big. They also eat slow-moving animals on the seabed, and can rip, shred and pierce flesh.

PESKY PLANTS

Not everything in the garden is rosy. Look hard enough and you will find plants that don't want to be eaten, so they fight back. These pesky plants have spines, prickles and poisons – and they are ready for battle.

STRENGTH IN NUMBERS

One way that plants can survive is by making sure there are lots of themselves! They can make thousands of seeds at a time, which means there is a good chance that lots of them will grow into new plants. If there are enough of them, they may smother other plants trying to grow nearby.

MEAT-EATERS

Most plants make their food using sunlight, but some peculiar types have come up with a better way to get food – they catch, grab or even drown small animals, and turn their bodies into a tasty bug soup.

WARNING!

TOXIC TERRORS

The nastiest of all plants are the ones that look harmless, but harbor foul poisons in their leaves, berries or flowers. These toxins may be so harmful they can make an animal or person ill just by touching the plant. If such toxins are swallowed, death often follows.

THORNS AND THISTLES

Most leaves are soft, juicy and tasty, and they make a great meal for a plant-eating animal. Some plants, however, defend themselves from attack by growing tough spines, thorns or prickles on their leaves or stems. Only animals with very thick lips will dare to munch on a mouthful of thistles or prickles.

63

POISONOUS PLANTS

Plants give us food, clothing and shelter, but some plants pack a powerful punch – their gruesome poisons can make us very sick… or worse!

DEAD MAN'S BELLS

Foxgloves look like perfect garden flowers, but their common name of dead man's bells gives a clue to their deadly nature. They have a poison that affects the heart, and can cause a heart attack. People have used them to make heart medicines – but also to commit murder!

SHRIEKING FREAKS

Long ago, witches grew mandrake plants for their spells – if the roots were eaten, they made people extremely ill, sleepy and confused. According to legend, mandrake roots scream when pulled from the ground, and anyone who hears the scream will die.

DEADLY BEANS

The deadliest plant in the world is the castor bean plant. As the large, spiny seed pods dry out in the sun, they split open and the beans shoot out with considerable force and fly through the air. The beans contain the poison ricin. Eating just a few beans would kill a person in minutes.

LETHAL LEAVES

Hemlocks look harmless, but some types are deadly to animals and humans. Victims can die agonizing deaths within just a few hours of eating the leaves.

Never eat the berries from a deadly nightshade plant. They contain a chemical called atropine that can cause breathing problems, terrible headaches and death.

AMAZING!

TOXIC TREE

The manchineel tree grows throughout the Florida Everglades, Central America and the Caribbean. Eating its fruit can kill you, smoke from burning its wood can cause blindness, and just standing under it in a rainstorm and getting splashed by the water running off its leaves can cause rashes and itching.

THORNS, SPINES AND PRICKLES

Sharp thorns and prickly spines can puncture skin, damage eyes and rip flesh. No wonder most animals won't eat them!

CUTTING EDGE

Many types of grass contain tiny spikes of glass, which is why they can rip your skin when you touch them. The glass in the leaves is designed to put animals off eating the grass, as it wears away teeth very fast. Animals that do eat lots of grass either have very hard teeth or teeth that are constantly growing.

ANT HELPERS

Acacia trees rely on their thorns to keep lots of animals away, but elephants and giraffes have such tough skin and tongues that they don't mind the prickles. To keep these big nibblers at bay, the trees make little berries on their leaves that ants eat, and in return the ants bite the trunks and noses of giraffes and elephants, which stops them eating the trees.

Cacti grow in hot, dry places where there is little food for grazing animals to eat. Their green stems store water, and their leaves grow as prickly spines to stop animals eating them.

STABBING PLANTS

Thorns are sharp and strong. If an animal rubs against a thorn, or tries eating a thorny plant, the sharp tips can break off, get stuck inside the animal's flesh and cause pain or infection. Some tropical palms grow very long spines on their leaves. The plants quickly grow to 18 m (60 ft) tall or more, and then drop their heavy, spiny leaves, impaling any creature (or person) who happens to be underneath.

COOL FACT!

HAIRY MARY!

Roses often grow thorns, but their prickly parts don't compare with those of the hairy mary plant. This plant has unbelievable thorns that can grow as long as a hand!

STINKY PLANTS

Imagine the smell of rotting socks, foul drains, dead bodies and sweaty gym shoes. These are just some of the disgusting smells that plants can make.

STINKY TREAT

Orangutans love to dine on durian fruit. The smell from this juicy stinker has been described as a mix between rotting fish and poo, but lots of jungle animals adore it. They know that the stink comes from the prickly rind, and that the fleshy fruit inside is soft, juicy and very tasty.

PUTRID PONG

Flies like to lay their eggs on rotting flesh, so it's no wonder they like the smell of the dead horse arum lily. This plant not only stinks like a putrid corpse, but it also gives off heat. The heat makes the pong spread far and wide, which helps to attract flies from farther away.

UPSIDE-DOWN TREE

The freaky-looking baobab tree is also called the upside-down tree, because when bare, its huge trunk and thick branches look more like roots. Baobabs have huge, white flowers that smell quite sweet until they turn brown, when they start to stink. The rotting, musty smell attracts bats, which pollinate the flowers.

CORPSE FLOWER

Plants need insects to help them grow seeds. To attract them, some plants make sweet smells, while others make a foul stink. Titan arum flowers, known in Indonesia as "corpse flowers," smell of rotting meat, and that's a smell that lots of flies find too tempting to resist. The flowers grow to a record-breaking 3 m (10 ft) tall, so their stench can spread far across the forest.

DID YOU KNOW?

STRANGE SMELLS

A titan arum's foul smell can make people nearby feel sick, but other arums smell of bananas or freshly chopped carrots.

69

FLESH-EATING PLANTS

Most plants make their own food, but some prefer to "eat" food, and they have some gross ways of getting their meals!

SCAN ME
Instructions on page 5

SNAP TRAPS

The Venus flytrap is the most famous of all mean, green, meat-eating plants. When a fly lands on the soft, fleshy "traps," it can wander about happily… until it touches one of the trigger hairs. Then, slam! The trap shuts, capturing the fly inside, and its body is soon turned into a juicy, gloopy mush.

STICKY TRICKS

The pretty red stalks on this sundew plant are tipped with glue. Bugs land on the stalks, thinking they are in for a treat of sugary nectar, but instead find themselves trapped. The more they wriggle, the faster they stick.

FLY SOUP

The long cups on pitcher plants are made from rolled-up leaves. Flies are tempted into the cups by their bright colors and sweet smells. Inside the cups, the flies drown in a pool of water and flesh-dissolving chemicals. The plant then absorbs the goodness from the "fly soup."

AMAZING!

FROGS' FEET

Some pitcher plants get extra goodness from animal droppings that fall in to their cups. Others trap frogs and turn them into frog soup. All that remains of the frogs are their slippers! For some reason, the skin on frogs' feet doesn't dissolve.

COOL FACT!

NICE AND SLOW

It can take up to 10 days for a Venus flytrap to digest its meal.

QUICK AS A FLASH

Bladderworts grow in ponds and are the fastest killers in the animal kingdom. Their traps can slam shut on a mosquito larva in less than 1/50th of a second.

STINGERS AND STRANGLERS

Some plants have weapons to defend themselves against animal attack. Others attack and kill other plants.

A strangler fig grows up and around another rainforest tree, slowly strangling it to death. After the big tree has died and rotted away, the strangler fig is left standing as a hollow tower.

DON'T TOUCH!

The leaves of stinging nettles are armed with tiny hairs tipped with beads of glass (silica). When a hair is touched, the glass breaks off and the end of the hair injects a cocktail of poisons. Some of the chemicals give you pain, some make your skin itchy and swollen, and others make the pain and itchiness worse!

LIGHT ALERT

The sap of the giant hogweed plant, which is often grown in parks and gardens in Europe and North America, can give you a nasty rash and blisters that scar for years. However, the sting only takes effect if you touch the plant and then let the sun shine on your skin.

DON'T LOOK NOW!

The blinding tree, or "blind your eye," grows in mangrove forests and swamps in many tropical parts of the world. The sap from the blinding tree can make a person go blind. Every part of the plant is poisonous and must not be eaten.

RUNAWAY ROOTS

Like a massive, slow-moving monster, this huge tree (Tetrameles nudiflora) is slowly taking over the Ta Prohm temple ruins in Cambodia, Southeast Asia. The giant buttress roots of this type of tree can be up to 6 m (20 ft) tall, while the tree itself can reach a staggering 45 m (147 ft) tall – about as tall as 26 men standing on each other's shoulders!

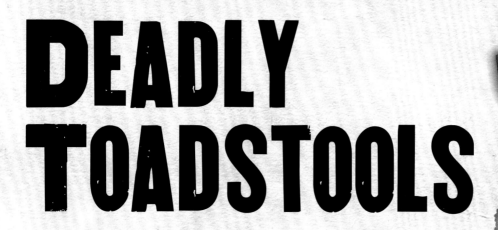

DEADLY TOADSTOOLS

Do you think mushrooms and toadstools are plants? Think again, because they are more like animals. They belong in a group of living things called fungi (say fun-ghee).

WHY ISN'T A FUNGUS A PLANT?

Fungi do not make their own food. They feed on other living things, or on dead animals and plants.

OBSCURE ORIGINS

Toadstools and mushrooms are the same thing – they are the parts of a fungus in which the spores (seeds) grow. The word "toadstool" dates back to the 14th century, and is generally used to mean a poisonous mushroom. Toads were regarded as being very poisonous.

Death caps look very similar to mushrooms that are fine to eat, and that spells bad news for mushroom pickers. Eating just half of a death cap mushroom would be enough to kill an adult.

ANGEL OF DEATH

The pretty white caps of this toadstool look like little umbrellas – but this fungus is called the "angel of death," and with a name like that you know it's best to stay away from it! Eating it can have deadly results. First a victim is violently ill and empties out his guts. Then his liver is slowly destroyed. The chances of survival are small.

RED FOR DANGER!

The red cap of this toadstool spells danger. It is a fly agaric, and it is packed with poison. Anyone who eats a fly agaric will find that the poison makes them sweat and dribble – a lot! It also makes them confused, and they may imagine seeing things that aren't really there.

DID YOU KNOW?

FACT FILE

We have tiny fungi growing on our skin. Sometimes they grow too much and cause foul skin conditions, such as athlete's foot.

Mold is a type of fungus. It makes bread go green, apples rot and turns old meat toxic and smelly.

Fly agarics were once used to make a potion for killing flies and other insects.

BULGY BODIES

Have you got the stomach for an in-depth look at the horrible human body? Prepare to be amazed at some of the gruesome and gross things that go on under and on your skin. Here are a few tasters to get you in the mood!

PAIN FREE BRAIN

The human brain doesn't feel any pain, which is why brain surgeons can operate on a patient while they are still awake. Long ago, people with bad headaches were sometimes persuaded by "doctors" to have holes drilled in their skulls, so the pain could escape. Amazingly, some of the patients survived!

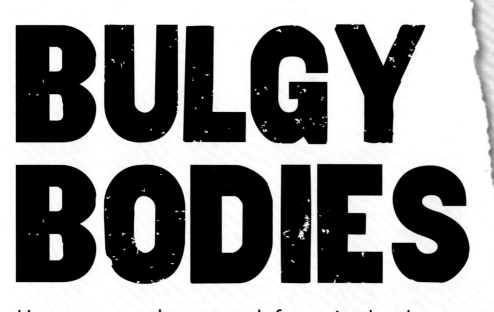

BROWN OR GREEN?

Everyone knows that poo is brown, so why do young babies have yellow or green poo? Poo turns brown in our guts because old, dead, red blood cells and a dark liquid called bile are added into the mix. Babies don't have many old blood cells to get rid of yet, so their poo stays pale.

There are tiny bugs, called mites, living at the base of your eyelashes! They are actually useful, as they eat any bacteria that want to make a home around your eyes.

NO SMELL

About two in every 100 people have no sense of smell at all. Scientists have found that girls are better at smelling than boys!

DiD YOU KNOW?

TOILET TIME

You can expect to spend about six months of your life on the toilet.

SEE YOU LATER

Why do people rub their eyes when they wake up in the morning? This simple movement helps to shift all the gunk that has settled on them over night – old tears, dead skin from the surface of your eyelids, snot and dirt. Thankfully, you don't need to wash your eyeballs because a steady flow of tears keeps them clean when you are awake.

BRAIN POWER

Your soft, wrinkly brain may not look like much, but it controls all of your body and everything you do.

SOFT AS SPONGE

A brain has two halves, and a wrinkly outer layer, called the cortex, which is divided into lobes. The cortex is wrinkled so that we can fit more brain cells into the head. Brain cells are called neurons. When a baby is still in its mother's tummy, it can grow up to 250,000 new neurons every minute!

BRAIN PARTS

Thinking happens in the front lobe.

Collecting information on touch, taste and pain happens in the parietal lobe.

Muscles are controlled in the cerebellum.

The brain turns information from the eyes into pictures in the occipital lobe.

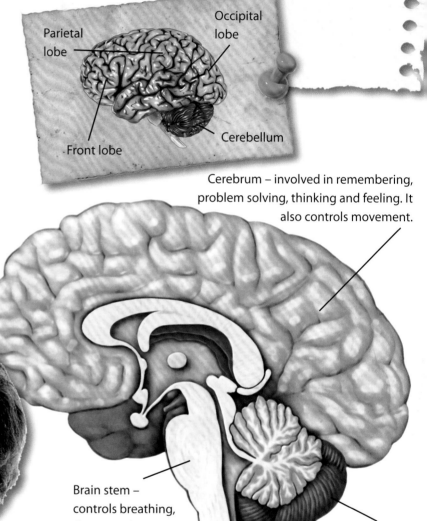

Parietal lobe

Occipital lobe

Front lobe

Cerebellum

Cerebrum – involved in remembering, problem solving, thinking and feeling. It also controls movement.

Brain stem – controls breathing, digestion, heart rate and blood pressure

Cerebellum – controls coordination and balance

CANNIBAL KILLER

Kuru, or laughing sickness, is a brain disease that makes people chuckle, but it's no laughing matter as kuru is a killer. Like mad cow disease, kuru is caught by eating brains from other animals. Its victims were cannibals who got it from eating other humans, rather than infected cows!

Brain injuries can affect people's behavior in strange ways. One 10-year-old British girl banged her head and began to write upside-down and backwards. When she banged it again a year later, her writing returned to normal!

BRAIN FREEZE

Have you ever suffered from "brain freeze"? You get this shocking pain from eating something cold. The sudden cold sends your brain into panic-mode as it tries to warm you up, and that sets off lots of pain-maker cells in your head. Luckily, brain freeze is harmless and it only lasts about 10 seconds.

DID YOU KNOW?

BRAIN FACT FILE

Weight	3 lb (1.4 kg)
Water content	78%
Number of neurons	100 billion
Data handling	70,000 thoughts a day
Memory storage	100 trillion facts in a lifetime
Energy use	20% of all body energy

BLOOD AND BONES

The human body sometimes suffers some gruesome wounds, but it has an amazing ability to heal itself.

BILLIONS OF BEATS

If you die at the age of 75, your busy heart will have beaten about 3 billion times. It beats at least once a second, sending blood around your body and back to your lungs to pick up more life-giving oxygen. A body holds about 5 litres (1 gallon) of blood. Each day, about 15,000 litres (3,300 gallons) of blood pass through the heart.

SCABS AND CLOTS

When you cut your skin and begin to bleed, your body swings into action. The blood vessels shrink to slow the bleeding, and tiny blood cells rush to the wound to seal it by forming a plug or clot. White blood cells also storm the wound, killing any bacteria.

JELLY BONES

Bones aren't all hard – they have a soft, spongy bit inside, called the marrow, which looks a bit like jelly. Bone marrow makes 173 billion new blood cells EVERY DAY!

IN A TWIST

People with flexible joints can turn their bodies back to front, bend their fingers right back and pull their arms out of their sockets. Gross!

DID YOU KNOW?

SNAPPING BONES

If you break a bone, blood will flow into the broken bit and form a clot. Soft cartilage, which is like bendy bone, grows over the break, and new bone begins to set. The break can be repaired in less than six weeks.

SQUISHY NOSE

Your nose is made of cartilage, not hard bone, and that's why you can squish it with your fingers.

DISAPPEARING BONES

Babies have about 300 bones, but there are 206 bones in an adult body, connected by 400 joints. Do babies lose 94 bones? No, their bones just fuse together to make fewer bones.

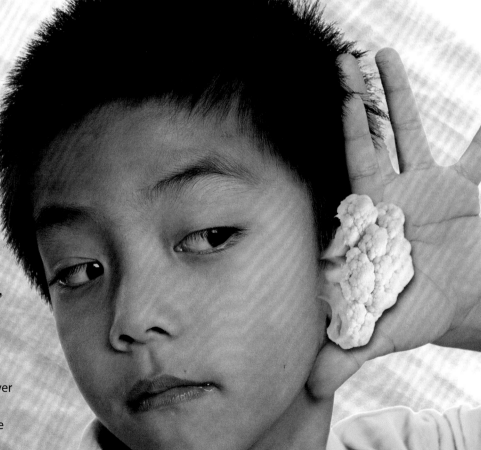

VEGGIE HEAD

Scars form when a wound is too deep to heal with a simple scab. Repeated wounds to one area of the body can cause life-long damage, such as cauliflower ear. This is a condition in which the ear develops nasty lumps and bumps that won't go away. People who play contact sports are most at risk.

TONGUE–TWISTER

Stick your tongue out, look in the mirror and be impressed! There's more to a pink, spit-covered tongue than you might have imagined!

BUMPY BUDS

Your tongue is the first line of defence against gruesome bugs and bad tastes. It is covered with about 10,000 tiny taste buds, and each one has up to 100 special taste-sensing cells. The taste buds for bitterness are near the back of the tongue, and help to keep us alive; things that are very bitter or sour may be poisonous, and the bitterness makes us want to spit food out, or even vomit!

11A

12

11A

12

TRY THIS!

Eight muscles in your tongue move it up and down, sideways, in and out and help you shape it so you can speak. This is why phrases that are tricky to say are called "tongue-twisters." Try this one – it's said to be the hardest tongue-twister in the world: The sixth sick sheikh's sixth sheep's sick.

DID YOU KNOW?

SUPER SPIT

Your mouth makes 1 to 2 litres (2 to 4 pints) of saliva a day! The saliva washes around your tongue and teeth, breaking down food and washing away old food and bacteria. Most of it gets swallowed – that's 50,000 litres (13,200 US gallons) in a lifetime – enough to fill a swimming pool!

A pink tongue is a healthy tongue, but it can turn yellow if old food and germs collect on it. Some bacteria that grow on tongues are the same ones that make teeth rot and fall out!

MEOW

About 2,500 years ago in Assyria, criminals had their tongues cut out and fed to the king's cats. This is the origin of the phrase "Has the cat got your tongue?" – a question people ask to someone who is silent when they are expected to speak.

DIGESTION

One enormous tube runs through your body, from your mouth to your bottom. It takes food on an amazing journey of disgusting digestion.

WE NEED FOOD

You are what you eat, but the reason you don't look like burger and fries or slippery noodles is that your body does a magical trick with food and turns it into something else. This process takes place in your digestive system, where food is broken down and turned into energy and stuff to repair your body and help it grow. Poo is what's left over!

BIG BURPS!

Look out! Gas is brewing, stewing and fizzing in your gut. As the bubbles grow there's only one way for them to go – up and out! We burp when gases build up in our stomachs after swallowing air during a meal, or from drinking fizzy drinks. A burp is noisy because the gas makes the seal between your stomach and throat vibrate. Unfortunately, if that seal is weak you may bring up some food with a burp, and that's sick.

AMAZING!

MMM, TASTY!

Intestine and stomach walls are covered with a thick slime to stop them from digesting themselves. Even so, one million stomach cells are turned into stomach soup every minute.

GRUESOME GUTS

Your intestines, or guts, are the long, sausage-like tubes that run from your stomach to your bottom. They are 8 m (26 ft) long, which is hard to imagine when you look at your belly! The intestines are where the gruesome job of making poo takes place. First, all the goodness is taken out of the food as it passes through, and then the waste is passed out of your tail end about 12 hours after your meal.

GROWLING

Sometimes your stomach makes an embarrassing rumbling or growling noise. This happens when pockets of air and gas get squeezed along with the gooey mix of food in your digestive system.

SOUPY STOMACH

Once food is swallowed, it is forced down into the stomach, where a foul soup of burning acid awaits it. The stomach churns the food around every 20 seconds or so, making slurpy noises as it mixes it in with the acid. This mashes the food, so it's small and soft enough to go on to the guts.

85

SKIN TROUBLE

What would we look like without skin? This amazing stuff keeps our insides safe inside us and keeps the dirty world out.

SMELLY FEET!

If you could see your skin close-up, you'd find about 1,000 different species of bacteria living on it. The bacteria on our feet eat our sweat – each foot produces more than 0.5 litre (1 pint) of sweat a day – and this creates an acid that causes foot odor.

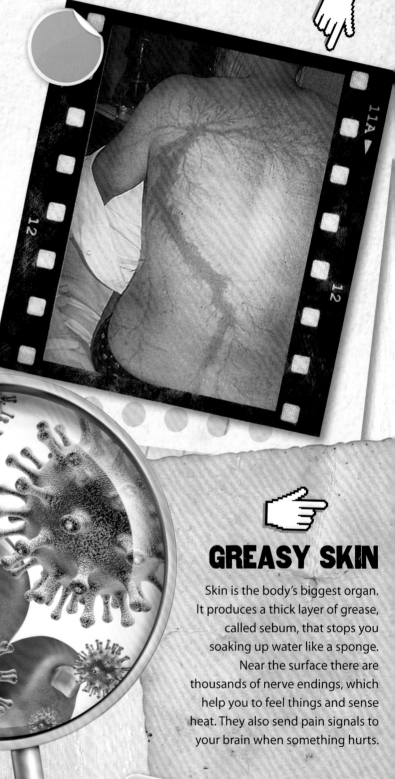

LIGHTNING STRIKES

People unlucky enough to have been hit by lightning (but lucky enough to have survived) are sometimes left with weird burn patterns on their skin. These flowery red marks are called Lichtenberg figures. They are caused by little blood vessels breaking under the skin.

GREASY SKIN

Skin is the body's biggest organ. It produces a thick layer of grease, called sebum, that stops you soaking up water like a sponge. Near the surface there are thousands of nerve endings, which help you to feel things and sense heat. They also send pain signals to your brain when something hurts.

DiD YOU KNOW?

If you could peel off an adult's skin and spread it out flat, you'd find it measured about 2 sq m (22 sq ft). Just one piece the size of a postage stamp contains 1,000 nerve endings.

DEAD SKIN

You lose about 10 billion flakes of skin every single day! Over a lifetime, this adds up to 20 kg (44 lb) of dead skin.

OUCH!

Spending too long in the sun is a bad idea – those rays are ultra-powerful and packed with burning radiation. The result can be sunburn, which leaves skin sore and red, then blistered and peeling. Gross!

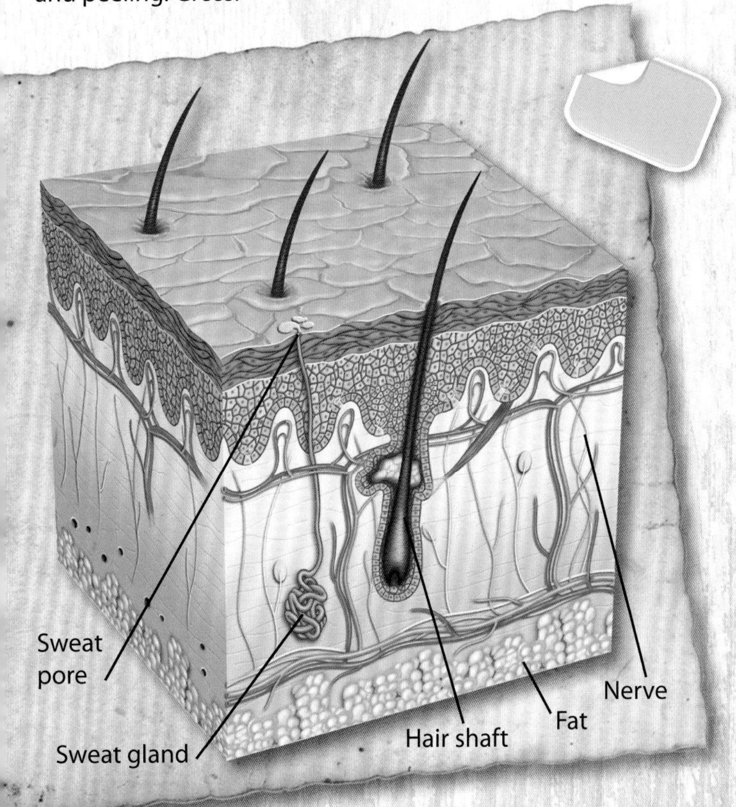

Sweat pore

Sweat gland

Hair shaft

Fat

Nerve

ZITS, BOILS AND SORES

As well as beastly bacteria, the skin plays host to viruses and tiny fungi, too, and these can cause us no end of trouble!

TERRIBLE TEENS

When children begin to turn into adults, they start to grow thicker hair – and more of it – and their skin makes extra sebum. The thicker hairs and greasy sebum block up the tiny holes (pores) in the skin, and that's when the zit trouble begins!

WARTS

Viruses are the zombies of the natural world because they are sort of alive, but not quite, and they are difficult to destroy! Warts are caused by viruses that make the skin grow into lots of rough, hard layers that build up into big bumps. They are harmless, but annoying. Warts that grow on feet are called verrucas.

AMAZING!

ACNE DIARY

1. Sweat and sebum block up the skin's tiny pores and can't escape. They build up under the skin, forming little bumps.

2. Bacteria start to feast. (If no bacteria feed on the sebum, you get a blackhead.)

3. An infection builds up, and the bumps turn into mini-volcanoes – spots, or zits!

4. White blood cells storm in to kill the bacteria, and make lots of oozy, gloopy pus.

5. Pressure builds up and the zit erupts, forcing out the bacteria, blood and pus. Gross!

BURSTING BOILS

When bacteria build up around the root of a hair, they can cause a red swelling, called a boil, under the skin – and it hurts! Pus collects for up to three weeks before the boil bursts. Sometimes people get a cluster of boils, called a carbuncle.

DID YOU KNOW?

FOUL FUNGI

The fungi that grow on skin can only be seen with a microscope – until they get a growth spurt and cause an infection. Ringworm and athlete's foot are gruesome skin infections caused by foul fungi.

Viruses cause cold sores. These are painful blisters on the lips. They are really easy to catch, so people with cold sores have to give up kissing for a while!

FEELING FUZZY

Your head is spinning and you can feel the contents of your belly heading north. Your body is in a state of sickening panic, and there's nothing you can do!

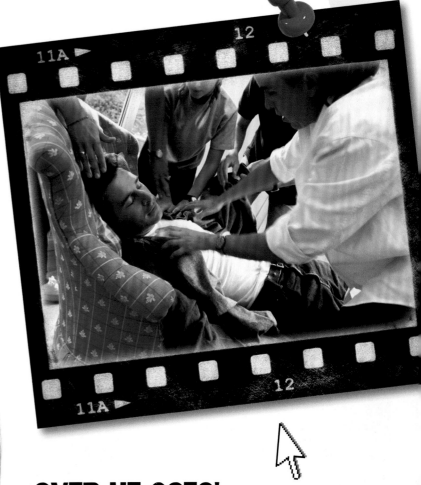

OVER HE GOES!

If you have ever fainted, you probably felt sick or dizzy first, as the blood drained away from your face. Sweat broke out on your brow, your legs went weak – and then you fell. People faint because blood stops going to their brain for a few seconds. This can happen for lots of reasons: sudden pain, shock, laughing, sneezing, getting too hot, terrible pain, or standing up for too long.

CHUCK-UP OR UP-CHUCK?

There are many gruesome names for vomiting: puking, chucking-up (or up-chucking!), chundering, heaving, getting sick, barfing ... the list goes on. A stomach chucks out its contents when it doesn't want it any more, often because there's something toxic in there. Food poisoning bugs irritate the stomach walls, which make the muscles around the stomach tighten. This forces a half-mashed gloop of lumpy food and liquid up and out of the mouth.

DIZZY SPELLS

Your body knows which way is up because you have organs of balance in your inner ears. These are called the semi-circular canals, and they are liquid-filled tubes. If you tilt your head, the liquid tilts too, and a message about the movement zaps over to your brain. Your brain also uses information from your eyes and your muscles to help it work out where and how you are moving. When these messages get muddled, you feel dizzy and sick.

SPACE SICKNESS

Astronauts often get space-sickness as they learn to adapt to weightlessness. There is no gravity in space, and that can really confuse a human body. Whenever they wear their space suits, they are given anti-nausea patches to wear, to stop them vomiting, because vomiting in a spacesuit could be fatal.

TURNING GREEN

Your bulging brain has a lot of work to do most of the time, but taking it on a boat trip is no break. Suddenly, your brain gets a whole load of confusing messages telling it that the world is tilting and sliding. If it gets too muddled, you start vomiting! Infections in your inner ear can have the same effect.

91

THE SMELLY BITS

Let's face it, most of the odors that come from a person's body don't smell too good!

CHEESY SHOES

The palms of our hands and soles of our feet make lots of sweat. If we trap the sweat on our feet in socks and shoes, we are creating the perfect place for bacteria to grow and make our feet smelly. Some things increase the amount we sweat, such as exercise, eating curry and drinking tea or coffee – but there's one part of us that never sweats – our lips!

DOG BREATH

Eating garlic and onions can make your breath smell of... garlic and onions! Real bad breath is much nastier, because it's mostly caused by bacteria farts! The bacteria feed on leftover bits of food stuck between teeth and on the tongue, and they make foul-smelling gases.

WHO DID THAT?

As food travels through the guts, it's worked on by helpful bacteria that break it down so that the body can take out the goodness. Unfortunately, the bacteria make lots of gas while they work, and that gas has to escape. When it leaves the body, the gas often makes a loud noise and a foul smell – and that's a fart!

ARMPIT DISASTER

Sweat cools us down as it evaporates on our skin, but under our arms it gets trapped. Bacteria thrive in this dark, damp environment, and start to break the sweat down. It's this breakdown that creates an unpleasant smell. If we wash the bacteria off, we wash the smell away, too.

COOL FACT!

DON'T TRY THIS!

Farts contain a gas called methane. It burns really easily if you set a match to it (but we don't recommend you try this at home!)

93

SNOTTY NOSES

Those little green blobs of slimy or crumbly snot that your finger enjoys hunting for up your nose are actually lumps of mucus mixed with dirt and old skin.

MILK ALERT!

Drinking milk can make some people produce more mucus. It triggers a reflex reaction in the body. But it won't actually make your cold worse!

SLIMY MUCUS

Every day, the cells that line the inside of your nose secrete about four cups of mucus. You may blow out a little of this onto a tissue, but most of it you swallow without noticing! When you get a cold, the amount of mucus increases greatly, and it thickens and turns from clear to white, yellow or green.

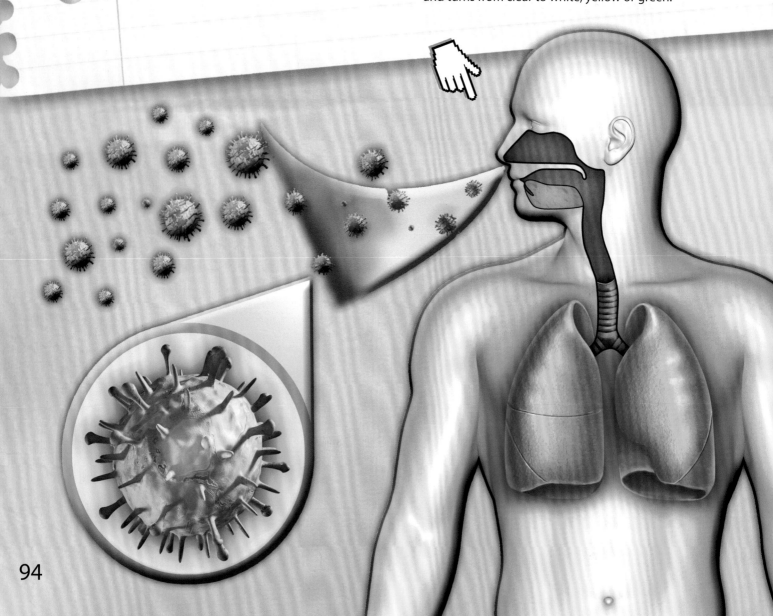

EYE GUNK

When you wake up, do you like to pick out the blobs of white or greenish mucus from the corner of your eyes? Known as "sleep" or "eye crusties," this discharge is a mixture of dust, blood cells, skin cells and thin mucus. During the day, it is washed away by tears and blinking, but at night it collects and hardens into "eye boogers."

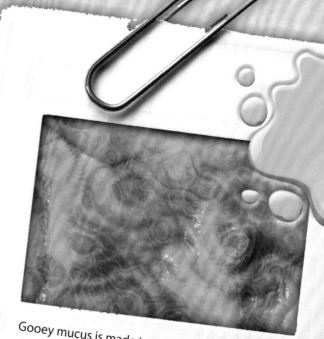

Gooey mucus is made in the membranes that line the mouth, nose, sinuses, throat and the passage that extends to the base of the lungs.

SNOTTY SNACK

70 out of 100 people admit to picking their noses. Gross! Out of those 70 people, 30 people admit to eating their boogers.

Eating snot isn't actually harmful, because it can strengthen your immune system. However, the bacteria on your hands and fingers aren't an ideal snack! If you need to get rid of your snot, use a tissue and don't forget to bin it!

NOT ALL BAD

Mucus looks disgusting, smells a bit weird, and picking it is gross – but it's actually good for you! It keeps your nasal passages moist so they work properly, and helps to protect you from infections by trapping bacteria, dust and pollen so they don't reach your lungs. Usually it kills the bacteria and viruses that it traps – but an allergy or cold can throw your body's mucus production into overdrive.

COUGHS AND SNEEZES

The old saying goes "Coughs and sneezes spread diseases," and it's as true today as it ever was. Coughing and sneezing can also stop you from getting ill.

THE BIG SNEEZE

When tiny bits of dust or dirt get up your nose, they can tickle, and that triggers a sneeze. You close your throat, then open it as the air in your lungs flies out. Your tongue goes back to block off your mouth, and all the air is forced out of your nose at a super speed of 161 km/h (100 mph). The dirt is carried out with the air, leaving your nose nice and clean.

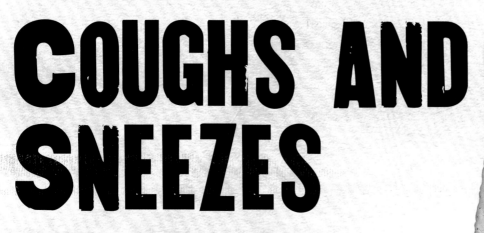

VILE VIRUSES

When you sneeze, the air that flies out of your nose carries mucus, slime and snot from the inside of your nose. If your sneezing was triggered by a cold, then the snot spray will spread vile viruses everywhere it touches.

STUCK SNEEZING

In the 1980s, a schoolgirl sneezed every five minutes for 978 days. She sneezed more than one million times in the first year.

FLOWER POWER

Flowers make pollen, a yellow dust that they need to grow seeds. If you are allergic to pollen, you get hayfever. The pollen irritates the lining of your nose, which makes more mucus, and you end up with a runny nose, sneezing and red, itchy eyes.

When you cough, you force air through your airways, helping to clear them. If you've got a cold, though, coughing helps the virus that caused the cold to get into someone else's body. So cover your mouth with a tissue when you cough!

COOL FACT!

COMMON COLD

There are more than 200 types of virus that could be to blame for a common cold.

HIDEOUS HAIR

Long, short, curly, straight, thick or thin – this strange stuff grows all over our bodies, and it stands on end when we are scared.

BODY HAIR

Armpit and other body hair has a shorter life than head hair, which is why it doesn't grow so long. Each strand of hair grows out of a group of hair cells, called a follicle. Curly hair grows out of hair follicles that are asymmetrical (oddly-shaped) while straight hair grows from hair follicles that are symmetrical (evenly-shaped).

WHAT A SHOCK

People often say that someone's hair "turned white overnight" after they had a shock, such as a bereavement. Hair doesn't actually turn white with shock, but stress and fear can make colored hairs fall out, leaving just white hairs behind.

GRAY DAY

As people get older, the cells that make hair color begin to die. Once they have died, a hair grows out white, and lots of white hairs make all the hair look gray.

GROWTH

It takes a month for a strand of hair to grow just 1 cm (0.4 in.). It grows for up to seven years before falling out.

DARK OR FAIR?

Hair is colored by a pigment called melanin. There are two types of hair melanin – dark (brown-black) and light (red-yellow). All hair colors are made from these pigments.

HAIRY FACES

Some women grow thick, dark hair on their faces, and can even produce a full beard. Another hairy condition that people can suffer from is Ambras Syndrome, which causes hair to grow all over their face, including their nose. People who have this condition are sometimes cruelly called "wolf people."

HAIR FACTS

If you have fair hair, you probably have about 150,000 strands on your head. People with dark hair have about 100,000 strands, and redheads have the least - about 90,000 strands.

About 100 hairs a day fall out of a person's head. New ones grow in their place, unless the person is going bald!

A single hair is as strong as a piece of copper wire of the same thickness.

WHY DO BODIES HAVE THESE?

Here are some important questions about the body that you may have wondered about but never dared to ask!

HOW LONG WILL NAILS GROW?

Some people have grown their finger and toenails really long – the record for fingernails is about 8.5 m (28 ft)! Few of us could ever beat this, because our nails simply wear away or break off when they reach the end of our fingertips.

WHERE DO BELLY BUTTONS COME FROM?

Your belly button marks the spot where your umbilical cord was attached. This cord connected you to your mother's body when you were growing inside her. It carried everything you needed – such as food and oxygen – into your body.

WHAT ARE EYEBROWS FOR?

Eyebrows catch sweat that drips down our foreheads, and stop it getting into our eyes. They also give our eyes a little bit of protection from strong sunlight shining down from above.

DID YOU KNOW?

WHY DO I HAVE EARWAX?

Earwax collects in the ear canal, which connects the outside world to the hearing parts of the ear inside your head. It cleans the ear canal, and also makes it much harder for insects to crawl inside!

WHY IS SPIT IMPORTANT?

Spit, or saliva, is full of chemicals that begin to digest our food. It helps to break food into small enough chunks to swallow, and helps food slip gently down our throat without tearing its soft lining. Spit also helps to keep our teeth clean, and helps us to talk.

DEADLY DISEASES

If you have lumps, bumps, rashes or a fever, it could be a sign that you have a deadly disease.

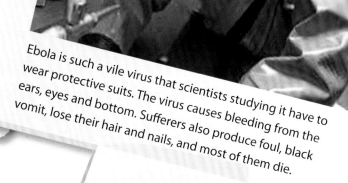

Ebola is such a vile virus that scientists studying it have to wear protective suits. The virus causes bleeding from the ears, eyes and bottom. Sufferers also produce foul, black vomit, lose their hair and nails, and most of them die.

AMAZING!

ERADICATED – ALMOST!

Smallpox is caused by a virus. It used to be very common and killed millions of people. No one gets it any more because doctors and scientists succeeded in wiping it off the face of the Earth – almost! They keep some bits of smallpox in bottles, stored in a very safe place, just in case they ever want to do more experiments on it.

RED RASHES

Measles is spread by sneezes. It is a virus that causes headaches, fever, red eyes and a nasty red, itchy rash that can cover the whole body. In many parts of the world, young children are injected with a vaccine that gives them long-lasting protection from the disease.

PUTRID POO

If your poo goes from solid to liquid, and then from brown to yellow... beware! These are symptoms of cholera. If it goes untreated, you can die, because you will begin pooing out bits of your gut, and all the liquid your body contains. Cholera is caused by bacteria that live in dirty water, and it's still common in many parts of the world.

BEASTLY BUGS

Malaria is one of the world's deadliest diseases. It's carried by female mosquitoes, which bite people to suck their blood. Bacteria live in the mosquitoes' spit and carry the malaria disease from person to person. It's more often fatal in children.

MORE DEADLY DISEASES

Deadly diseases can spread quickly, causing people to have gruesome symptoms and die agonizing deaths.

PLAGUE VICTIMS

The plague is rare nowadays, but it has caused hundreds of millions of deaths in the past. Victims get ill, coughing up their lungs, developing big black lumps under the skin and bleeding from every hole. Sufferers can die a terrible death within just four days of catching plague. In the 17th and 18th centuries, plague doctors wore beak-like masks filled with herbs to protect them from the putrid air that they believed was a cause of the plague.

MAD AND BAD

If you hate baths and often have spit dribbling out of your mouth, you are exhibiting two signs of rabies – a foul disease that is caught when an animal infected with rabies bites you. It affects the brain, driving you crazy and making it unbearably painful to swallow, which leads to a fear of water.

BAD BACTERIA

Known as the Black Death, plague is caused by bacteria that live inside rat fleas, but it easily spreads to people. Once a person has the plague, the bacteria grow quickly in their blood. Within a few days they may have a billion bacteria in every drop of blood.

Tetanus bacteria make a deadly toxin that makes muscles contract and jaws freeze, which is why the disease is sometimes called lockjaw. You can get it from puncture wounds, such as those made by rusty nails.

SCURVY

What happens if you don't eat fruit and vegetables? Your teeth fall out, your skin can turn purple and yellow, you get very sick with an illness called scurvy, and then you die! Why? Because fruit and vegetables contain Vitamin C, which your body needs to make collagen – the really important stuff that holds your bones and skin together.

COOL FACT!

POOR DIET

Sailors suffered from scurvy when they were at sea, because a diet of rum and maggot-filled biscuits was low in Vitamin C. Often the sailors got better when they were given lemon or lime juice to drink, or fresh fruit to eat.

TOOTHACHE!

Long ago, people thought rotten teeth were being eaten by a tooth worm! The truth is different, but just as gruesome.

DID YOU KNOW?

HOW MANY?

Humans have two sets of teeth. They grow their first set of 20 as children, and these are gradually replaced by the second set of 32 teeth. Some adults grow fewer than 32 because they don't have wisdom teeth. The best way to keep your teeth until old age is to keep them clean. That means brushing them at least twice a day, flossing them and drinking water.

TOP TIPS FOR TOOTH-ROT

If you want to have painful teeth, fillings, gum disease and eventually have all your teeth removed, we recommend that you:

Drink lots of sugary, fizzy drinks.
Eat lots of sweets.
Eat white bread.
Never brush your teeth.
Never visit a dentist.
Drink lots of fruit juice.
Suck on lemon wedges.

FOLK REMEDIES

In the days before most people could afford a doctor, folk remedies were often used to try and relieve pain. A 19th-century cure for toothache involved hammering a nail into the tooth until it bled, and then hammering the nail to a tree to transfer the pain. To prevent toothache, people would tie a dead mole around their neck!

AMAZING!

CLEANING RECIPES

In Roman times, people looked after their gums by rubbing them with the ashes of burnt mice heads, rabbits' heads, wolves' heads, ox heels and goats' feet. They even used old wee as a mouthwash – now that's really gross!

BUGS IN THE MOUTH

The food in your mouth isn't just a meal for you – millions of bacteria eat it too! They nestle in the cracks between your teeth and near your gums, and create a nasty layer of goo, called plaque. As they eat the food they find in your mouth, the bacteria ooze an acid liquid that burns through the protective layer of enamel on your teeth and makes holes in it.

DID YOU KNOW?

KILLING THE WORM

Long ago, people believed that tooth pain was caused by a worm, and that the best way to cure it was to kill the worm. Various gruesome methods were used, such as chewing chilli, popping a caterpillar into the mouth and even spitting into a frog's mouth!

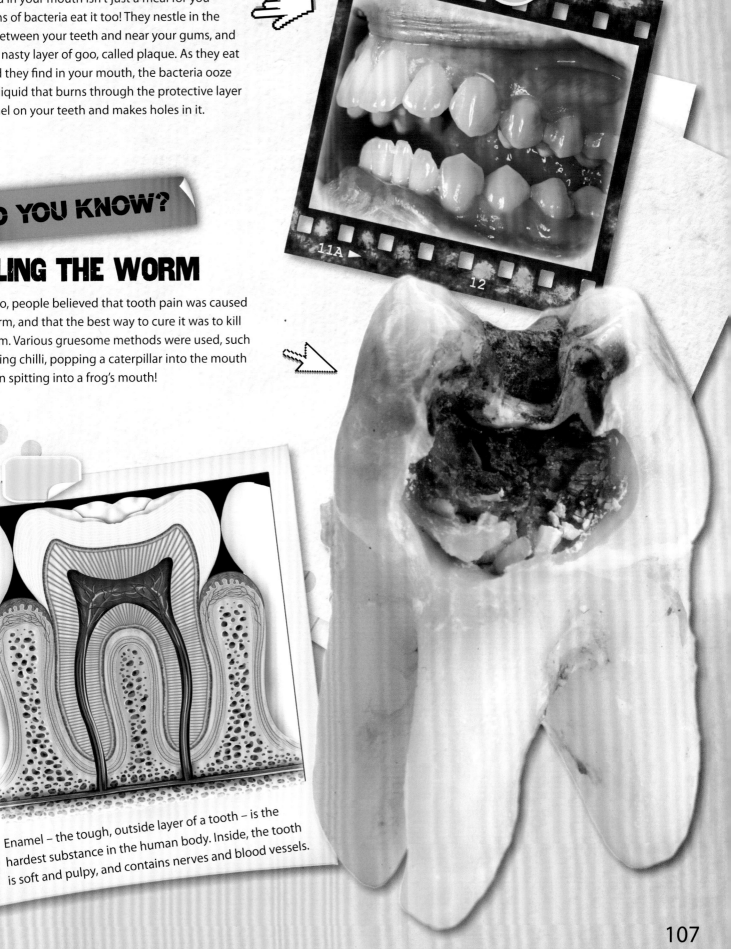

Enamel – the tough, outside layer of a tooth – is the hardest substance in the human body. Inside, the tooth is soft and pulpy, and contains nerves and blood vessels.

HISTORY'S HORRORS

History is full of stories to make our hair stand on end. In every age things went on that were not just horrible to live through, but are almost as gruesome to read about later!

STONY SECRETS

The ancient stones of Stonehenge were never bloodstained by ritual slaughter, so far as we know. But Bronze Age graves close by hid some grisly secrets: a girl's skull split by an ax – could this have been a sacrifice? – and a man shot with arrows, hurriedly buried – was this murder or execution?

In Medieval times, humiliating an offender by exposing them to public scorn and ridicule was an important part of their punishment. Pillories were set up in public places, so people could jeer at the criminal, as well as throw things at them.

GORY GREEKS

The ancient Greeks excelled at coming up with gruesome tales of brutal battles, angry gods, malevolent monsters and terrible torments. Prometheus, for example, was a mythical Greek hero punished by the gods for stealing fire for human use. He was bound to a rock, and each day had his liver torn out by an eagle.

BLOODY BATTLES

All battles are bloody, but medieval battles could be stomach-churning. Swords were used to lop off arms, arrows pierced skulls and spears were thrust through armor. A swipe from the ax of a Viking or Saxon warrior could split a man from head to thigh.

STRICTLY SPARTAN

The Spartans lived in southern Greece, and liked nothing better than going to war. They became the dominant military force in Greece about 650 BC.

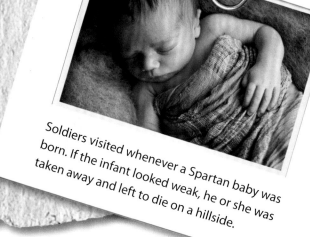

Soldiers visited whenever a Spartan baby was born. If the infant looked weak, he or she was taken away and left to die on a hillside.

A SOLDIER'S LIFE

Every Spartan was expected to have a perfect body. Warriors spent most of their time keeping fit. A Spartan soldier wore his hair long. Before battle, he combed his hair and put on a red cloak, so blood would not show.

BODY BEAUTIFUL

Spartan girls wrestled, did gymnastics and practised combat skills. They wore short skirts to run in, and had more freedom than other Greek girls. The Spartans believed that healthy women produced strong babies, and that meant more Spartan soldiers.

HOW COOL!

STEALING

Boys were taught that it was fine to steal food, so long as they did not get caught. If a boy was caught, he was beaten, so that he would learn to be smarter next time. Boys were flogged in religious temples to show the gods how tough they were. To cry was considered a sign of weakness.

AMAZING FACT

MONEY MAKES MUSCLES

One way to keep fit was to carry Spartan money about. The Spartans sneered at the pocket-sized coins of other Greeks. Their cash came in the form of heavy iron bars, as long as a walking stick.

TOUGH TRAINING

Spartan boys started training to be soldiers from age 7, when they were taken from their mothers and sent to army barracks. There they lived, trained and slept together. The boys learned how to find food, how to march, run and climb barefoot, how to swim and how to fight with swords and spears.

GORY GLADIATORS

Imagine being sent out in front of a yelling crowd to kill someone – or get killed! That was the fate of a gladiator in ancient Rome.

SWORD SWAP

A gladiator with a sword might fight an unarmed opponent. If he won, he had to fight next time without a sword.

KILLING SCHOOLS

Gladiators were trained in special fighting schools. Most were prisoners-of-war, criminals or slaves. Some gladiators wore armor so heavy they could hardly walk. Others fought almost naked. There were a few women fighters, too.

NO PAPER!

Nervous gladiators probably needed the toilet before a fight. The Romans did not use toilet paper. Instead they used a water-soaked sponge on the end of a stick!

FIGHTER'S FOOD

In training, gladiators ate mostly starchy foods and vegetables. Trainers fed them spoonfuls of ash to make their bones stronger.

CHOOSE YOUR WEAPON

Some gladiators were chasers – they ran around the arena with a sword and shield. Some had two swords. A tricky fighter was the *retiarius*, who threw a net to entangle his opponent, then stabbed him with a long, three-pronged fork, called a trident.

All gladiators swore to fight to the death. If a fighter tried to run away, the crowd would jeer. He might then be tortured to amuse them, before being killed.

THUMB SIGNAL

If a gladiator was wounded and the crowd wanted him to live, they would wave their scarves and hands. The emperor then signaled his fate, but no one is sure whether he put his thumb up or down if the gladiator was to die. If the sign was "die," the wounded man was killed and his body dragged out of the arena.

FIGHTING BLIND

Roman crowds always liked something new. Sometimes a gladiator was pitched against a bear or a tiger. Sometimes two gangs of gladiators fought each other. A gladiator might even be made to wear a helmet with no eye holes, so he could not see what he was trying to hit.

113

GRUESOME GAMES

Bloodthirsty Roman crowds enjoyed wild beast shows and "games," in which thousands of animals and people were killed in an arena.

CHARIOT RACING

The Romans loved to watch chariot races, held on an oval track. Desperate to win, drivers would flail their whips and recklessly cut across their rivals. If a chariot overturned, the driver would be flung out and crushed beneath the wheels or hooves of the other chariots as they thundered past – to the delighted shrieks of the crowd.

AMAZING!

MASS SLAUGHTER

Roman games were "killing Olympics," staged by emperors to celebrate wars, to show off and to win popularity. In AD 108–109, Emperor Trajan staged games that lasted for 123 days, during which 9,000 gladiators and 11,000 wild animals were slaughtered.

WATCH OUT!

FED TO LIONS

Persecuted Christians were first paraded around a Roman arena, mocked, stripped naked, and then left to face hungry lions, which were released to maul and kill them.

ANIMAL COMBAT

Roman crowds cheered and yelled as they watched animals fight to the death. They craved new thrills: a bear fighting a buffalo, a lion against a bull, a rhino against an elephant. In one gory spectacle, 500 human gladiators fought 20 elephants.

SAFARI SPECTACLES

Roman spectators could buy tickets to hunt animals in the arena, which was turned into a mock jungle for the occasion, with trees and even lakes. On these "safari hunts," the ticket showed which type of animal the hunter was allowed to kill. At one games in AD 80, 5,000 wild beasts were killed in one day.

Bullfighting became a popular alternative to gladiator combats. Today, bullfights are still held in Spain and Mexico.

CRAZY CALIGULA

The Roman emperor Caligula staged spectacular shows with wild animals. On one occasion he decided to feed the animals with criminals, because butcher's meat was too expensive. He also loved horse racing, and even considered making his favorite racehorse, Incitatus, a consul. The horse's oats were mixed with flakes of gold, and it had a marble stable and an ivory manger.

115

HORRID ROMAN HABITS

Rich Romans enjoyed the good life, but some Roman habits and tastes seem gruesome to us today. They could be quite disgusting!

SNAIL DELIGHT

The Romans liked to fatten snails on a diet of milk and salt, and then fry them as a delicacy. Snails are still a popular dish in France.

YOU MUST BE JOKING!

Roman cooks amused dinner guests by creating joke dishes, for example by serving up a roast hare with birds' wings attached, to make it look like a miniature Pegasus (the fabled winged horse). A favorite titbit was a dormouse, stuffed or dipped in honey and rolled in poppyseeds.

HUMAN CANDLES

The emperor Nero regularly held vile orgies at his palace, the Golden House, in Rome. Here, guests were given special bowls to vomit into after they had eaten to excess. They were also made to witness one of his most barbaric acts. Nero had Christian prisoners tied to wooden stakes, smeared with tar and set alight to burn as human candles.

The Romans had a favorite sauce, which was found in almost every kitchen. It was made from smelly fish guts that were salted and dried in the sun.

DID YOU KNOW?

LETHAL LEAD

The Romans liked to drink wine sweetened with a syrup, called *defrutum*, which was made from grapes fermented in lead pots. Lead also leached from the glazes of pottery and from lead piping used to carry water. Many Romans suffered from severe lead-poisoning as a result. Symptoms included painful gout and even madness.

WASH DAY

People in ancient times did not have washing powder. Instead, they made soap from ashes, and collected wee in pots to use on wash day, as a soaking bleach to whiten clothes. Wee was also used by leather-makers, who collected it by the cartload.

SLAVES AND PERSECUTION

The Roman world had few machines, so slaves were made to do much of the heavy work. If they ran away or broke Roman laws, they faced terrible punishments.

PERSECUTION

Christians who refused to accept that Emperor Nero was a god were hunted like criminals. Hundreds of Christians were put to death, and Church leaders, including Peter and Paul, were killed. Peter was crucified upside down. Paul, because he was a Roman citizen, had a swifter death and was probably beheaded.

SOLD!

Slaves played an important part in Roman society, and some had highly skilled jobs. They had no legal rights, however, and were considered the property of their owner, who could sell them at market. A few hard-up Roman citizens even sold their own children as slaves to make a bit of extra money.

SCAN ME
Instructions on page 5

ROW HARDER

The Romans enslaved their foreign prisoners-of-war. Some were sent in chains to row the galleys of the Roman fleet, and others were made to work in the mines. Either at sea or underground, few survived for long.

GRIM REVENGE

In 71 BC, a slave and former gladiator named Spartacus led a slave uprising against the Romans. After the revolt was finally put down, 6,000 captured slaves were crucified. They were suspended from wooden crosses along the Appian Way (the road to Rome), and were left dangling for all to see. Such gruesome scenes were repeated during the persecution of the Christians by Emperor Nero.

Unlucky slaves had cruel owners who whipped them and gave them little food. Runaway slaves were chased and killed.

DID YOU KNOW?

DEATH ON A CROSS

Crucifixion was a terrible way to die. Captives sometimes had nails hammered through their feet and wrists to hold them to the cross, and death was slow. The victims usually died from asphyxiation as their lungs collapsed, but sometimes a soldier stabbed them or broke their legs, which helped them to die more quickly.

AMAZING!

CONDEMNED

In AD 61, politician Lucius Pedanius Secundus was murdered by one of his slaves. As a punishment and warning to others, the Senate, led by Cassius Longinus, said that all 400 slaves of the dead man must die. Emperor Nero approved the decision.

BLUE WARRIORS

The Celts lived in Europe from about 600 BC. They are remembered for being fierce warriors. Some charged into battle dressed only in blue warpaint (made from plant dye) to show how brave they were.

DID YOU KNOW?

BOG BODY

In 1984, a body was discovered in a dried-up bog near Manchester, England. "Lindow Man," as it was called, was the victim of Celtic ritual sacrifice. Some 2,000 years earlier, he had been drugged, knocked out, strangled, stabbed and then thrown into a pool.

BAGGY TROUSERS

The Celts liked bright clothes patterned with checks and stripes, similar to Scottish tartan. The men often wore a cloak, tunic and trousers, and a neck ring, or torc, made of gold or silver. They carried a long, double-edged sword, a spear and a decorated shield for protection.

BOUDICCA

In AD 61, Queen Boudicca of the Iceni (a tribe in East Anglia) led an army of British Celts against the Romans. She destroyed Roman London. Skulls found in the River Thames are thought to have belonged to people slaughtered by Boudicca and her army. The Romans eventually defeated her, butchering 80,000 Celts. Rather than be paraded in chains as a captive, Boudicca killed herself.

TOO FAT TO FIGHT

The Celts believed it was very important to keep fit. Men were punished if they got too fat to charge into battle waving a spear and sword.

CARRIED AWAY

Celtic women fought in battle, served as priestesses and ruled as queens. However, with at least ten kinds of lawful marriage, a man could have several wives, or kidnap a woman and carry her off.

COOL FACT!

BURNED ALIVE

At the Celtic spring festival of Beltane, people lit great bonfires and sometimes drove cattle through the flames to protect them from disease. They even burned prisoners alive inside wicker figures.

PUNK HAIR

To make themselves look scarier, some Celtic warriors washed their hair with lime or clay to bleach it and make it stand up in spikes. Others bleached it and combed it back so that it looked like the mane of a running horse.

It was once thought that Stonehenge, in England, was built by Celtic high priests (Druids), but it is now known that it pre-dates the Celts by several thousand years.

VILLAINOUS VIKINGS

Vikings were expert sailors who traveled thousands of miles from home and gained a reputation for fighting, raiding and trading.

WELL NAMED

Erik Bloodax was a ferocious Viking warrior. His father, Harald Fairhair (who had 20 sons) was king of Norway for a short time from 930. Another Viking, Ivar the Boneless, was probably unable to walk, and was carried about on a litter or a shield.

GONE BERSERK

Vikings known as Berserkers charged into battle as if crazy, dressed only in animal skins. The name is possibly derived from a Viking word meaning "bare of shirt." Berserkers were said to bite their shields and eat hot coals, and they fought in such a frenzy that they stopped only when killed. Today, the phrase "to go berserk" still means to behave in a crazy, out-of-control way.

Vikings fought with a sword, ax or spear. Bows and arrows were also used, but it was thought braver to kill an enemy in hand-to-hand combat.

NAME THE DAY

Tuesday is named for the Viking god of the sky and war, known as Tyr in Scandinavia and Tiw in England. Wednesday is named for the chief god, Odin (or Woden in England). Frigg, or Freya, the goddess of love and the home, gave her name to Friday.

Tuesday

CHEERS!

After victory, it was once thought that Vikings drank blood out of human skulls. The toast "Skol!" may be derived from this gruesome custom. However, no skull cups have ever been found, so it's more likely they drank from cow-horn cups. They didn't wear horned helmets either!

DID YOU KNOW?

SNAKE PIT

The Viking chief Ragnar Lothbrok (Shaggy-breeks) is said to have been killed in a pit of poisonous snakes on the orders of King Aella of Northumbria. Ivar the Boneless later had Aella put to death in a very gruesome way by having his lungs pulled out through his ribs.

BRING ME BONES!

Vikings used bones for all sorts of things. The thin bones from a bird's foot were used to make needles for sewing. Horse and cattle bones were shaped into ice skates and tied to the bottom of shoes. Whale bones were even used to make "ironing boards" – fabric was smoothed on the boards using a glass weight.

AMAZING!

FIRE FROM WEE!

Vikings used wee (urine) to start fires! First, they gathered touchwood fungus from trees, crushed it into a felt-like material, charred it with fire and then boiled it in wee. Sodium nitrite from the wee made the touchwood slowly smolder but not burn, which meant fire could be transported safely, even on board wooden ships.

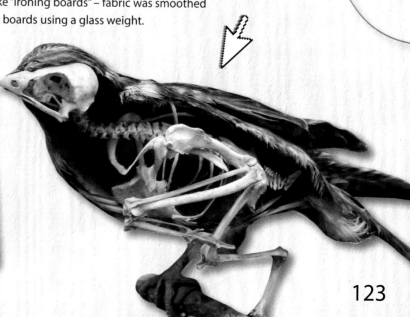

123

MEDIEVAL MISERY

Life was tough in Medieval times. Homes were cold, the streets stank, disease was a constant concern and punishments were harsh.

DOG AND DUCK

Medieval inns named "the Dog and Duck" held gruesome duck-baiting events. A duck with a clipped wing was released onto a pond, where it was chased by dogs. Its only escape was to dive under water. The owner of the dog that caught the duck in the least amount of time got a prize. If the duck escaped, the dog's owner had to pay the local innkeeper.

In medieval France, pigs were arrested for "breaking the law" and were flogged in public. In 1394, a pig was even hanged for murder.

DID YOU KNOW?

GRIM PRISON

The most feared London jail in the Middle Ages was Newgate Prison. People called it "a tomb for the living." Prisoners were chained together in damp, dark, cold cells with no heat, no bedding and no toilets. More people died there from sickness than were ever hanged.

ORDEAL BY FIRE

A person accused of a crime might be made to suffer an "ordeal by fire." This involved walking three steps carrying a piece of red-hot iron. The person's hand was then bandaged. If, after three days, the skin had not blistered, the person was judged to be innocent, but if there were blisters, the accused was found guilty and likely put to death.

DID YOU KNOW?

PUBLIC HUMILIATION

A fish-seller accused of selling rotten fish had to walk about with a stinking dead fish tied around his neck. A bad baker was dragged about on a wooden sledge, while a bad priest had to sit on a horse facing the tail and wearing a paper crown, while people jeered at him.

AMAZING!

DIRTY STREETS

The streets of Medieval towns were not places to linger! There was no sewage system, so toilet waste was simply thrown out onto the streets – the stench would have knocked you over! Rotten food was also thrown out, to be eaten by roaming pigs or the numerous rats. Not surprisingly, life expectancy for a poor person in a town was short.

TOOTHACHE

Toothache was a real misery in Medieval times. With no effective painkillers, people suffered in agony. When they could stand it no longer, they had their rotten teeth yanked out by tooth-pullers, who did a roaring trade at the weekly markets.

GARGOYLES AND GROTESQUES

Medieval churches are adorned with grotesque stone faces. The ones on the outside of buildings are gargoyles, concealing water spouts.

The Green Man, with leaves growing from his mouth, was originally a Celtic fertility god. He was adopted by the early Christian Church as a symbol of life, death an[d] rebirth, and can be seen on many Medieval churches

FANTASY ANIMALS

A typical gargoyle is a grinning demon with a gaping mouth. Some are shaped like fish, dragons or other fantasy animals. The mantichore had a lion's body, a human head with sharp teeth and a dragon's tail. Medieval artists sometimes got real and fantasy animals mixed up. Their "cameleopard" was a spotted camel – actually an attempt to draw a giraffe!

RUDE FACES

Medieval stonemasons were highly skilled craftsmen. They carved grotesques with scary, rude, weird or monstrous faces, and sometimes even copied the face of their boss or the local priest! Although they may look frivolous, the heads often had a structural purpose, helping to support the heavy arches above.

BUTLER

At Exeter College, Oxford, a set of modern stone carvings spell out the name of a college scholar, Marilyn Butler: marigold (M), archer (A), roundels (R), eye (I), lion (L), yew (Y), Neptune (N); then, bells (B), unicorn (U), twins (T), lamb (L), ear (E) and a Roman nose (R).

Rainwater issues from a gargoyle's mouth onto passersby below. The word "gargoyle" comes from an old French word, meaning "throat."

DID YOU KNOW?

WHAT FOR?

Grotesque images had a serious point – to show the fallen nature of mankind, the beastly side of human nature and the hellish demons that people believed lay in wait for the wicked.

THE BLACK DEATH

From 1348 to 1350, a terrifying disease from Asia struck Europe. The Black Death caused people to die in their thousands. Often they were dead in just a few hours.

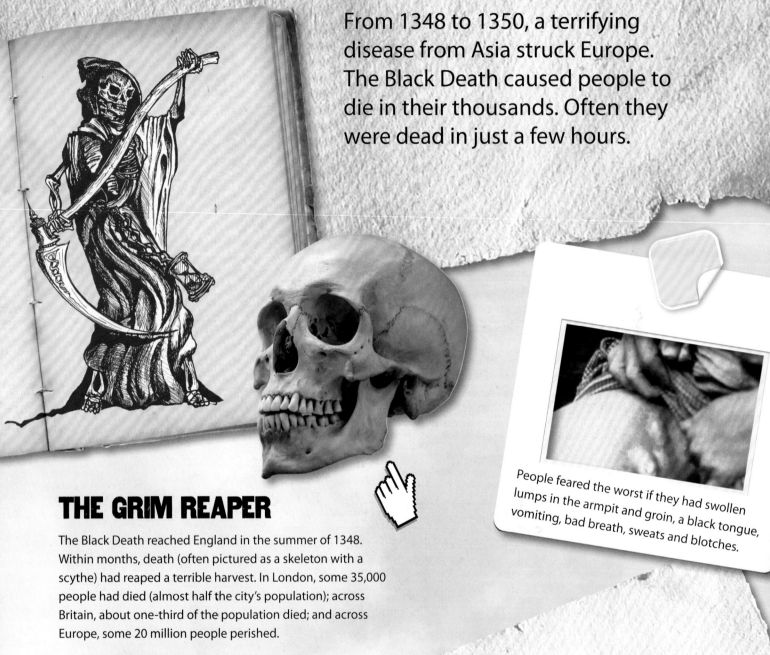

People feared the worst if they had swollen lumps in the armpit and groin, a black tongue, vomiting, bad breath, sweats and blotches.

THE GRIM REAPER

The Black Death reached England in the summer of 1348. Within months, death (often pictured as a skeleton with a scythe) had reaped a terrible harvest. In London, some 35,000 people had died (almost half the city's population); across Britain, about one-third of the population died; and across Europe, some 20 million people perished.

BEWARE THE RAT

The Black Death was spread by fleas that lived in the fur of black rats. Every Medieval town and village was alive with rats. The disease spread in other ways, too. When soldiers attacking the walled town of Kaffa in the Crimea started to die of plague, the survivors catapulted rotting corpses over the walls, so the infection spread to the defenders inside.

ABANDONED

In some villages, so many people died from plague that there was no-one left to plow the fields, grow the crops or look after the cattle and sheep. The few survivors simply had to abandon their homes and relocate to other villages.

In desperation, people tried all kinds of "cures" for the Black Death. One was to shave a chicken's bottom and strap it to the armpit where the tell-tale swellings first appeared.

PESTILENCE MEDICINE

Another "cure" was a potion made of egg shells, marigold leaves and petals, ale and treacle, warmed over a fire and drunk morning and night.

HELPFUL HERBS

Plague doctors wore beak-shaped masks stuffed with herbs to ward off the disease and mask the stench of dead bodies. They had no drugs to cure the plague, so they turned instead to spells and charms. Some tried drawing blood from the sick, or cutting out plague sores with a knife.

WITCHCRAFT

For hundreds of years, people lived in fear of witchcraft. Witches, wizards and warlocks were thought to use magic, for good and evil.

DEVIL WORSHIP

Secret signs, such as this pentacle symbol, were used by witches when they met together as a coven to do magic and worship the Devil. Covens often met on a Friday.

HANGED

Crimes of witchcraft included putting sickness spells on a person, or killing someone from a distance by making a wax effigy of them and sticking pins in it. The punishment was death. In England, witches were hanged. In Scotland and most of Europe, they were burnt at the stake.

HAMMER OF WITCHES

In 1486, a book called *Malleus Maleficarum (The Hammer of Witches)* was published by the Catholic Church. It argued that witches were real and dangerous, and told people how to hunt out and punish "suspects" – who were mostly harmless women.

SALEM WITCH TRIALS

In 1692, 19 people were hanged as witches in Salem, Massachusetts. Another was killed by being pressed to death with heavy stones. So ended the biggest witch hunt in American history. It had all begun when some teenage girls began acting oddly, rolling about, screaming and claiming they were bewitched.

DID YOU KNOW?

FAMILIARS

According to legend, a witch's familiar, or familiar spirit, was a supernatural being that kept a witch company and obeyed her commands. Traditionally, familiars took the form of an animal (usually a cat, dog, raven or toad). Some of the odd names they were given, such as Pyewacket and Vinegar Tom, were recorded in an English pamphlet of 1647.

THE PENDLE WITCHES

Twelve people who lived near Pendle Hill in Lancashire, England, were accused of being witches in 1612. Ten of them were found guilty and were hanged. They were accused of making cows sick, murder, conjuring up the Devil and keeping company with supernatural animal "familiars," such as black dogs.

DEADLY BREW

In Ireland, Alice Kyteler was accused of being a witch for killing three husbands and making the fourth sick. She was said to have fed them a brew that included dead men's nail clippings, the clothes, hair and brains of dead babies, a cock's intestines, spiders and black worms!

131

PUNISHMENTS

Punishments were often cruel and bloody. Painful torture was the fate of many prisoners in dark dungeons and loathsome cells.

IRON MAIDEN

The Iron Maiden looked a bit like a coffin or an Egyptian mummy case, but it was armed with vicious spikes. The helpless prisoner strapped inside would see the spikes closing in as the doors were shut. The iron maiden's final embrace was deadly!

TRAITORS ON SHOW

The heads of executed traitors were stuck on pikes (spearlike weapons) or poles for crows to peck at and crowds to mock. Guy Fawkes and the other Gunpowder plotters of 1605 ended up in this sorry state.

ON THE RACK

Invented in the 1400s, the rack was a torture instrument used in the Tower of London and other prisons to extract information. The victim was tied to a wooden frame by the arms and legs, and was painfully stretched until he gasped what his torturers wanted to hear – or until his bones and joints shattered.

DID YOU KNOW?

TRAPPED!

The Little Ease cell in the Tower of London was so small that a prisoner could not stand up or lie full length inside it without touching the walls or ceiling.

WATCH OUT!

THUMBS DOWN

Thumb screws were simple but effective. The victim's thumb was put into a clamp like a nutcracker, and was crushed. If he didn't talk, there was always the other thumb, and then the fingers...

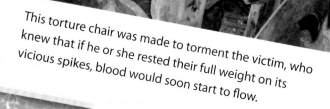

This torture chair was made to torment the victim, who knew that if he or she rested their full weight on its vicious spikes, blood would soon start to flow.

MORE PUNISHMENTS

Over the centuries, all kinds of gruesome devices were invented to punish offenders. A quick, painless death was seldom on offer.

CRUSHED!

Witches and heretics (people who offended religious teaching) were sometimes executed by being crushed to death. In this Chinese device, a giant millstone is lowered onto the victim, while hungry dogs wait to gobble up their remains.

DEATH BY A THOUSAND CUTS

One particularly gruesome method of Chinese torture and execution was called "death by a thousand cuts." It was used in China from about AD 900 to 1905, on people who had committed serious crimes, such as murdering their parents. The victim was tied to a stake in a public place, and flesh was sliced from their body for up to three days, so they slowly and painfully bled to death. Relatives might pay for a swift knife thrust to end the victim's agony.

Supplice chinois.

HANGED, DRAWN AND QUARTERED

From 1351, the punishment for treason was slow, painful and messy. The condemned man was dragged by a horse to the gallows, hanged until almost dead, then cut down alive ("drawn"). His insides were then cut out and burned, and his body was cut into four pieces, which were nailed up as a warning for all to see.

Petty criminals were clamped in a pillory, while onlookers jeered and threw rotten food at them.

AMAZING!

HEADS OFF

Decapitation, or beheading, was a method of execution used widely in Europe and Asia until the 20th century. In Britain it was reserved for people of noble birth. It was usually carried out with a sword or an ax. A skilled executioner could take off a victim's head with one blow. Anne Boleyn, Mary Queen of Scots, Lady Jane Grey, Sir Walter Raleigh and Charles I were all beheaded.

HAND OF GLORY

The corpse of a hanged highwayman was hung up by chains at a crossroads for all to see. Sometimes a thief would chop off the corpse's hand, and dry and pickle it so it could be used as a candlestick. A candle made from the fat of the same corpse and burned in the "hand of glory" was believed to give light only to the holder, so he could rob houses without being seen.

135

THE BLOODY MAYANS

The Maya ruled much of Central America and Mexico between AD 250 and 900.

ARROW SACRIFICE

In temples such as this one at Tikal, victims were sacrificed in the sacred arrow rite. The victim was tied to a stake and painted blue with a white target on his chest. Archers danced around him, shooting arrows until he was dead.

HEARTS

Cutting out human hearts was a religious ritual for the Mayans, who sacrificed their prisoners-of-war to the gods. A priest would use a flint knife to cut out the heart, which he would then hold up, still warm, to the crowd. Sometimes the corpse was skinned and the priest would wear the skin – now that's really gross!

DID YOU KNOW?

THROWN IN THE WELL

Human sacrifices to the Mayan rain god Chaac were thrown into well-like pits, known as sinkholes, or cenotes. In the Sacred Cenote at Chichen Itza – the great Mayan temple in southeast Mexico – archeologists have found human skeletons and sacrificial objects from these rituals.

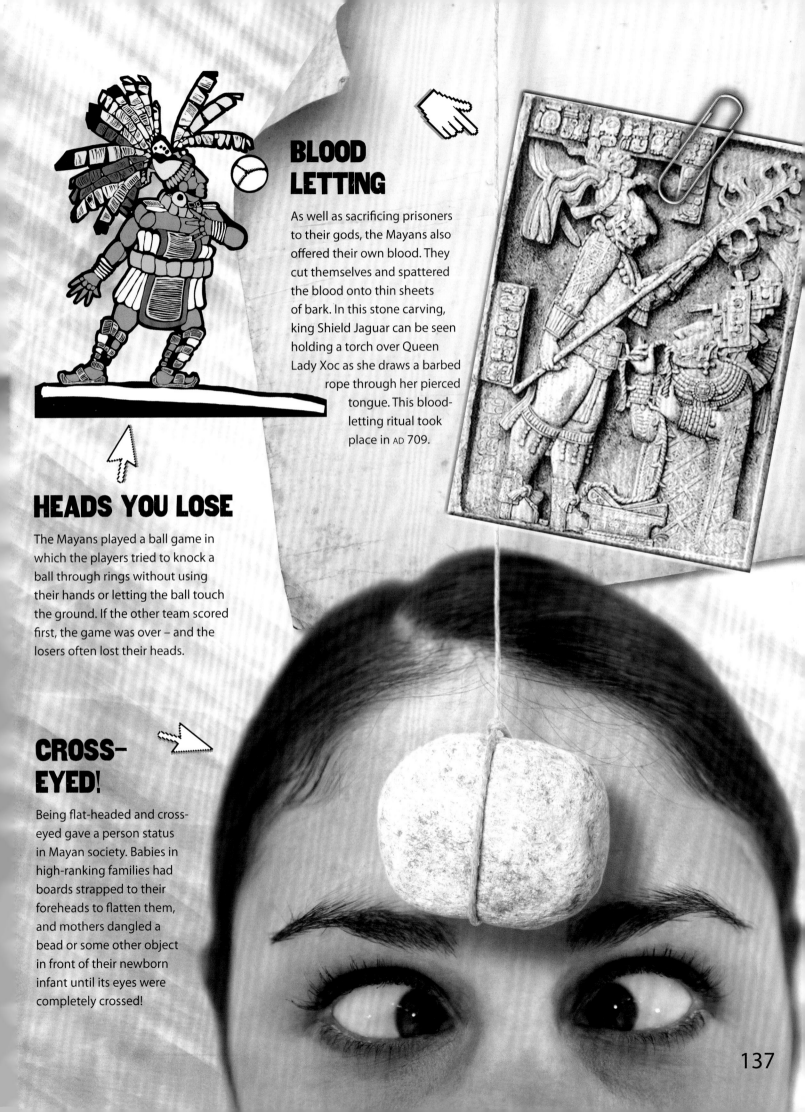

BLOOD LETTING

As well as sacrificing prisoners to their gods, the Mayans also offered their own blood. They cut themselves and spattered the blood onto thin sheets of bark. In this stone carving, king Shield Jaguar can be seen holding a torch over Queen Lady Xoc as she draws a barbed rope through her pierced tongue. This blood-letting ritual took place in AD 709.

HEADS YOU LOSE

The Mayans played a ball game in which the players tried to knock a ball through rings without using their hands or letting the ball touch the ground. If the other team scored first, the game was over – and the losers often lost their heads.

CROSS-EYED!

Being flat-headed and cross-eyed gave a person status in Mayan society. Babies in high-ranking families had boards strapped to their foreheads to flatten them, and mothers dangled a bead or some other object in front of their newborn infant until its eyes were completely crossed!

ANGRY AZTECS

The Aztecs ruled an empire in Mexico up until the early 1500s, when it was conquered by Spain. They were builders, warriors and artists, with some gruesome customs.

DID YOU KNOW?

MEXICO CITY

Today the vast mega-city of Mexico City sprawls above the remains of the Aztec city of Tenochtitlan.

JEWELS IN THE SKULL

The Aztecs kept human skulls on racks at their temples. They also used skulls in art, making jewel-encrusted and crystal skulls. This turquoise mask represents the god Tezcatlipoca, and has a skull as its base. Some people believe such skulls have mysterious supernatural powers.

Tenochtitlan was attacked and captured by the Spanish, led by Hernán Cortés, in 1521. They destroyed the city and many of its magnificent temples.

HUMAN SACRIFICE

The Aztecs had many gods, which they believed had to be fed with human hearts and blood. Prisoners were sacrificed on the steps of their towering temples. A priest would cut out a prisoner's heart, and sometimes people ate some of the flesh, too.

The Aztecs killed thousands of victims in their human sacrifice ceremonies. Walls of stone skulls remain as ghoulish reminders of this bloody past.

AMAZING!

DIE HARD

Tezcatlipoca was one of the most powerful Aztec gods. He was the god of night, sorcery and destiny. According to one legend, his sacrificial victims had to die fighting. They were tethered and given mock weapons, and had to fight to the death against four warriors dressed as jaguars and eagles.

WATCH OUT!

CHILD VICTIMS

One of the chief Aztec gods was the Sun-god Huitzilopochtli. To please him, Aztec priests would tear out a victim's heart and hold it up, warm and still beating, toward the sky. Most human sacrifices were slaves or captives, but children were killed as offerings to the rain-god, Tlaloc.

139

ELIZABETHAN HORRORS

Elizabeth I was England's queen from 1558 to 1603. She was highly intelligent, ruthless and had a fiery temper.

WIG MALFUNCTION

Mary Queen of Scots was kept prisoner in England by her cousin Elizabeth for almost 20 years, before she was finally executed for treason in 1587. As Mary put her head on the block, her pet dog hid under her dress. It took two strikes of the ax to sever her head. When the executioner picked it up, Mary's wig came off in his hand.

Elizabeth I wore thick white face paint, made of poisonous white lead and vinegar, to give her the fashionable pale look, and to cover her smallpox scars.

RUTHLESS QUEEN

Queen Elizabeth is said to have inherited her courage from her mother, Anne Boleyn, and her toughness and ruthless streak from her father, Henry VIII. When a group of plotters (the Babington plot) were captured, Elizabeth had them hanged, but before they were beheaded in the usual way, she ordered them to be cut down half dead and had them castrated and disemboweled.

NO MORE SUGAR!

Queen Elizabeth had an aquiline nose, reddish-gold hair, and was stately and regal in public – that is, until she smiled! Like many rich Elizabethans, she ate too much sugar, which was a luxury import, and had black teeth and gaps where rotten teeth had fallen out. Some people thought black teeth showed how successful they were!

COOL FACT!

RING DILEMMA

When, aged 69, Queen Elizabeth was dying, she had to have her coronation ring filed off because it was so embedded in her flesh. The ring passed to the new king, James VI of Scotland.

WHAT A WHIFF!

Elizabethans washed and swam, but did not believe daily baths were healthy. The queen had a proper bath only four times a year. Most ladies at court used lots of perfume, powder and makeup to help mask their bodily smells and grime.

STUART SCANDALS

Two major gruesome events took place during the Stuart period – the Great Plague (1665) and the Great Fire of London (1666).

THE GREAT PLAGUE

In 1665 London was hit by the Great Plague. By August, 1,000 people a day were dying, and bonfires filled the air with smoke to "cleanse" the pestilence. The Great Plague killed an estimated 100,000 people – about 15 percent of London's population.

SCAPEGOAT

A French watchmaker named Robert Hubert was hanged after he confessed to starting the Great Fire in 1666. However, it turned out that he was innocent and had only arrived in the city two days after the fire broke out.

DID YOU KNOW?

GREAT FIRE FACT FILE

The fire broke out on the night of September 2, 1666, at the home of Thomas Farynor, baker to King Charles II, in Pudding Lane.

It burned for five days, and destroyed:

13,200 houses
87 parish churches
3 city gates
4 bridges
1 prison
St Paul's Cathedral

100,000 people were left homeless.

No-one was killed directly by the fire.

SCAN
ME
Instructions on page 5

BRING OUT YOUR DEAD

Throughout 1665, the streets of London were filled with the noise of carts rumbling over the cobbles as men rang bells and shouted "bring out your dead." The city's graveyards soon filled up, so the bodies had to be carted off and buried in plague pits, or mass graves.

SIGN OF THE CROSS

A red cross was painted on the door of any house with a plague victim inside, and above it were written the words "Lord, have mercy upon us." By law, an infected house had to be shut up for 40 days, with all the members of the house inside. A watchman was posted outside to keep guard and make sure no-one came out.

FRENCH FRIGHTS

The years 1789 to 1815 were dramatic for France – first came the French Revolution, famed for its executions; then came the Emperor Napoleon, who fought endless battles.

OFF WITH HIS HEAD!

The French Revolution began in 1789, after a mob stormed the Bastille prison in Paris. The old government was overthrown, and France was torn apart as nobles fled abroad and people took to the streets. King Louis XVI was imprisoned in 1792, and beheaded on the guillotine in January 1793.

REIGN OF TERROR

The French Revolution turned really nasty in September 1793. In October, the revolutionaries, led by Maximilien de Robespierre, executed Queen Marie Antoinette, who they blamed for the country's financial problems. After the queen's execution, hundreds of other "enemies of the people" were sent to their deaths.

MADAME LA GUILLOTINE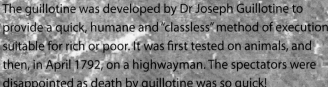

The guillotine was developed by Dr Joseph Guillotine to provide a quick, humane and "classless" method of execution, suitable for rich or poor. It was first tested on animals, and then, in April 1792, on a highwayman. The spectators were disappointed as death by guillotine was so quick!

DEATH OF ROBESPIERRE

Maximilien de Robespierre was the most bloodthirsty of all the French revolutionary leaders. He declared that even friends must die if they opposed the Revolution. When the order for his arrest was finally made, in July 1794, he tried to shoot himself, but managed instead to shatter his jaw. The next day, still bleeding and screaming as his bandages were torn off, he was guillotined.

HORSE MEAT

In 1812, the French emperor Napoleon Bonaparte led his army to invade Russia. He reached Moscow, but could not win a final victory. In the freezing Russian winter, more than 400,000 French soldiers either froze to death, died from sickness, or were captured. A few survived by gnawing flesh cut from still-living horses or the bodies of their dead comrades.

CHOPPED

As many as 30,000 people lost their heads on the guillotine in the bloody Reign of Terror.

POISONED!

After his final defeat in 1815, Napoleon was exiled to the island of St Helena. He died in 1821. At the time it was thought he died of cancer, but forensic tests have since revealed that his body contained large amounts of arsenic – possibly from his hair oil, from inhaling wallpaper fumes, or most likely from the hand of an assassin. The chief suspect is Charles Tristan, marquis de Montholon.

145

VICTORIANS UNVEILED

The Victorian Age (1837–1901) was an exciting time of change and inventions, but also one of dirt, disease and some gruesome customs!

DOG DIRT

Victorian dog-dirt collectors went around the streets picking up dog poop. They bagged up the poop for tanners (leather-makers), who mixed it with water to make a stinky brew, called "bate." This was used to turn cow and horse hides into soft leather.

UP THE CHIMNEY

Large Victorian houses had lots of fireplaces with sooty chimneys. Chimney sweeps sent small boys up the chimney flues to brush out the soot. The poor boys came out covered with soot, and often got sick. Even worse, some got stuck inside the chimneys and died there.

Bloodsports were popular spectator sports. A monkey named Jacco Maccaco of 1820s London was famous for killing dogs twice its size.

TOILET TROUBLE

Most Victorian homes had no indoor toilets. People had to go outside to an outhouse, or privy, where the toilet was just a seat over a hole in the ground that emptied into a cesspit.

THE GREAT STINK

In the early 1850s, the introduction of flush toilets to wealthier houses in London greatly increased the amount of sewage in the River Thames. During the hot summer of 1858, the smell became intolerable – it was called the Great Stink. Sewage, garbage and even dead animals filled the river, and MPs in Parliament had to put up chemical-soaked curtains to keep out the stench.

STUFF THAT!

Victorians loved to display stuffed animals in their homes. Some, such as little birds, were posed on branches under glass domes. Others were presented in a more comical way. A squirrel, for example, might be stuffed holding a cigar up to its mouth, and kittens were posed holding a tea party! Larger creatures included bears holding trays (like a waiter), lions and crocodiles, and stools were made from the feet of elephants.

147

SLUMS AND THE POOR

The poorest Victorians lived in gruesome slums. There might be as many as 19 people in two rooms, with everyone tipping toilet waste into the yard outside.

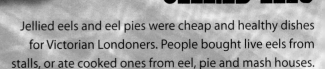

JELLIED EELS

Jellied eels and eel pies were cheap and healthy dishes for Victorian Londoners. People bought live eels from stalls, or ate cooked ones from eel, pie and mash houses.

STREET CRIME

Homeless children might be recruited by a "kidsman" (such as Fagin in Charles Dickens' novel *Oliver Twist*). He would train the children to work as pickpockets or house burglars, giving them food and shelter in exchange for stolen goods. Unwary visitors, drunken sailors and workmen who had just been paid might fall foul of "footpads" – muggers who would lie in wait, club them and then steal their money.

ANY OLD RAGS

One of the most hazardous of East End jobs involved collecting and sorting old rags for pulping into paper. Often the rags were scavenged, along with bones and other waste, and then sold to local traders. Workers risked being bitten by rats or infected by lice and fleas.

Charles Dickens's Dotheboys Hall, in his novel *Nicholas Nickleby*, was a horror-school of beatings and starvation – and some Victorian schools really were that bad. Before 1870, many children never went to school at all.

ROOKERIES

Tenements were lodging houses shared by lots of people. They had no proper kitchens, bathrooms or toilets. In London they were called "rookeries" (after the birds that nest together). One of the worst was St Giles, a notorious den of thieves. Charles Dickens had to be shown around by a policeman, as it wasn't safe to stroll there alone.

INFANT MORTALITY

Many women dreaded getting pregnant because it was common for mothers and babies to die in childbirth. Even if the babies survived into infancy, they were likely to die from childhood diseases, such as measles or scarlet fever. Parents might lose as many as five or six of their children.

DID YOU KNOW?

OLD NICK

One of the worst Victorian slums was London's Old Nichol or "Old Nick." A short walk from the Bank of England, it was a maze of narrow streets and crumbling tenements. One-quarter of all children born there died before their first birthday.

149

WEAPONS OF WAR

War is part of human history. From the earliest times, armies have used gruesome methods to win at all costs.

HEAD SLICER

Japanese Samurai warriors were proud of their long, curved swords. These had a steel cutting edge, but a softer iron core, so they didn't snap. A swordsman holding the sword in both hands could take off a head in one scything motion.

HORSE TRAPS

Soldiers on horses had an advantage over foot-soldiers, unless the foot-soldiers scattered caltrops. These were vicious iron spikes that stuck in a horse's hooves. They could do serious damage to soldiers' feet, too.

ASSAULT RIFLES

A handful of modern troops with assault rifles can do more damage than a whole army of soldiers with muskets. The FN-2000 is a state-of-the-art, gas operated, fully automatic assault rifle capable of firing grenades.

TERROR BUG

Anthrax is a dangerous bacterial disease, used as a terror-weapon, but banned by international agreement. It was used in biological warfare by Japan in Manchuria in the 1930s. During World War II, the Allies experimented with anthrax to kill cattle in Nazi Germany, but never used it. Anthrax spores sent in letters in the United States in 2001 caused a terrorist scare.

MORNING STAR

In Medieval battles, soldiers hacked with swords and axes, jabbed with long spears, or bashed their enemies' brains out with clubs. Even a knight wearing a helmet usually stayed down if thumped with a Morning Star – an iron club with a spiked, ball-shaped head!

STRANGE CUSTOMS

Human customs are often extreme, weird, gruesome or spooky. We like to scare ourselves, and each other!

DID YOU KNOW?

NOSE PLUGS

The women of the Apatani people, who live in the far northeast of India, used to tattoo their faces and wear round, bamboo plugs in pierced holes in the sides of their noses. They gradually increased the size of the plugs as they got older – some measure 2.5 cm (1 in.) across. Since the 1970s, younger women have stopped wearing the plugs.

MUD MEN

The Asaro people live in Papua New Guinea. At festivals, the men can be seen covered in pale mud, wearing monstrous masks of clay. This custom began long ago, when warriors, covered in mud from a battle, found that their sudden, ghostly appearance terrified the enemy.

Some cruel and gruesome practices are aimed at tourists, who are prepared to pay for hideous souvenirs. Frog purses, for example, are sold at many markets on Borneo and across the Philippines.

AMAZING!

CRAZY WORLD

It is all too easy for us to look at people living in remote parts of the world and find their customs extraordinary. But when we stop and think, it soon becomes clear that many of our own customs would seem just as outlandish to an outsider or to a time traveler seeing them for the first time.

NIFTY NOSES

Imagine how boring the world would be if we were all sensible and all the same! Every four years, the Dani people of Papua New Guinea hold a pig feast. Numerous pigs are shot at close range with bamboo arrows. Their tails are removed to be worn as magical neck ornaments, and the tusks are worn as impressive nose pieces. Such ceremonies, rituals and fashions make the world a more interesting place.

DEATH RITUALS

Funerals and cremations may involve strange rituals or unusual coffins, and in the past they have included some cruel ceremonies.

In Tibet, one Buddhist ritual involves cutting up the body of someone who has died and laying out the pieces for vultures to peck at.

FANTASY FUNERALS

Fancy coffins have become a feature of funerals in parts of the West African country of Ghana. A carpenter will build you a coffin to look like a jet plane, an elephant, an eagle, a fish, a racing car or even a giant cell phone. What a way to impress your friends when you go!

AMAZING!

ROYAL SACRIFICE

In ancient times, in parts of Europe and Asia, it was common for the servants and slaves of kings and queens to be sacrificed at a royal funeral, so that they could serve their rulers in the next world. The Great Death Pit at Ur, in ancient Iraq, contained 70 bodies.

MUMMIES

Dead bodies are sometimes specially preserved by drying, so that they do not rot. They are made into mummies, like this Egyptian one below. The earliest intact human mummy from Egypt dates back to 3400 BC. Even older deliberately mummified bodies have been found in South America. The Chinchorro mummies from northern Chile date from about 5050 BC.

Early in his reign, the Egyptian pharaoh Ramesses II started building a splendid memorial temple to himself, where people could worship him after his death.

CRUEL FLAMES

In the past, in India, wives would sometimes throw themselves on the fire when their husbands were cremated (they left their handprints before they went to their fiery death). This was called sati. The aim was to show how devoted they were. Sometimes they were forced to do it. Occasionally sati has happened in modern times, but strict laws now ban this cruel practice.

IN LOVING MEMORY

We may remember the dead with sadness or with respect – or because those who died chose bizarre ways to remind us of their lives.

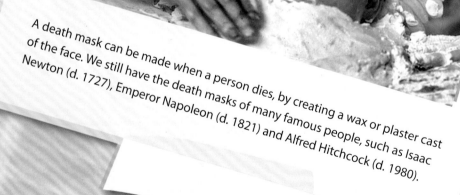

A death mask can be made when a person dies, by creating a wax or plaster cast of the face. We still have the death masks of many famous people, such as Isaac Newton (d. 1727), Emperor Napoleon (d. 1821) and Alfred Hitchcock (d. 1980).

DIAMONDS ARE FOREVER

Modern jewelers use carbon extracted from the ashes of the cremated body of a loved one, or from their hair, to make a diamond. This can be worn on a ring – at a cost of up to US$20,000!

BURIED UPSIDE DOWN

A memorial stone on Box Hill, near Dorking in England, marks the burial place of Major Peter Labelliere. He died in 1800 and was buried standing on his head. He had read that the world would be turned upside down on Judgement Day, and figured that when that day came, he would be the only person left standing the right way up!

KEPT ON SHOW

English eccentric Jeremy Bentham arranged for his body to be displayed after his death in 1832. His head was mummified and his skeleton was padded out with straw and dressed in his clothes. Later, a wax head was made. Since 1850, Jeremy has been on public display at University College, London. Sometimes he even attends meetings of the College – but they won't let him vote!

ROSEMARY

Throughout history, the herb rosemary has been linked with remembering the dead. It was strewn in graveyards so that its scent would mask the smell of rotting corpses. Some people came to believe that rosemary could preserve bodies. A sprig placed in the hands of a dead person would sometimes take root in the human remains and push upwards, breaking open the vault.

BARE BONES

Creepy skulls and bones are kept in stores beneath our cities, and are sometimes used as gruesome decorations!

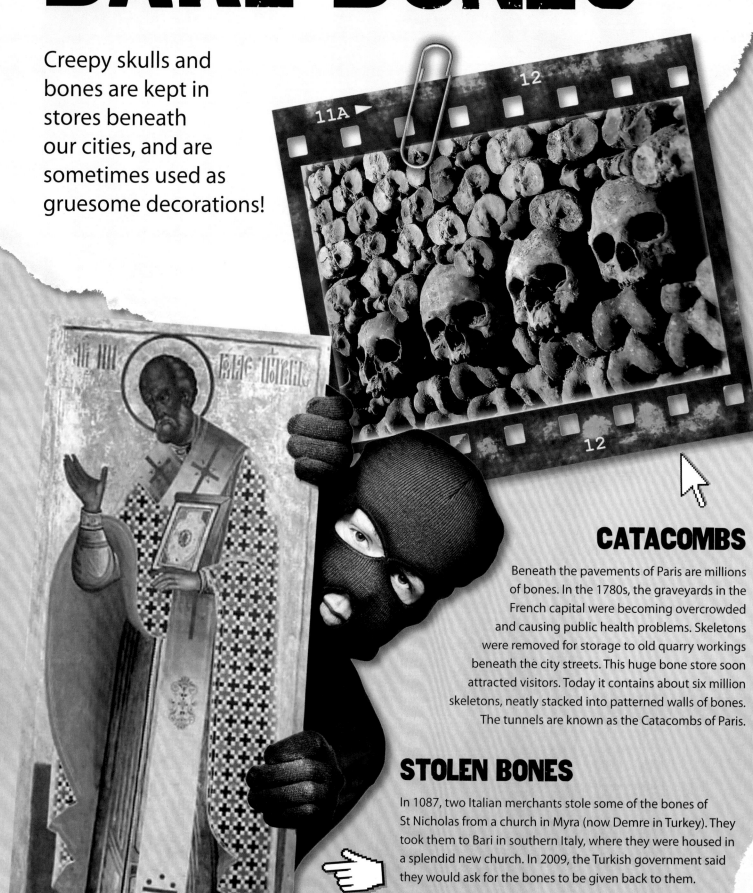

CATACOMBS

Beneath the pavements of Paris are millions of bones. In the 1780s, the graveyards in the French capital were becoming overcrowded and causing public health problems. Skeletons were removed for storage to old quarry workings beneath the city streets. This huge bone store soon attracted visitors. Today it contains about six million skeletons, neatly stacked into patterned walls of bones. The tunnels are known as the Catacombs of Paris.

STOLEN BONES

In 1087, two Italian merchants stole some of the bones of St Nicholas from a church in Myra (now Demre in Turkey). They took them to Bari in southern Italy, where they were housed in a splendid new church. In 2009, the Turkish government said they would ask for the bones to be given back to them.

CREEPY!

The Sedlec chapel in the Czech Republic dates back to the Middle Ages, and contains up to 70,000 skeletons. In the 1870s, the bones were arranged into spectacular pillars, garlands and even ornate chandeliers, used to decorate the chapel!

COOL FACT!

SKELETON STORES

Buildings where human bones are stored are also called ossuaries or charnel houses.

PLAGUE PIT

Sometimes diggers at building sites in European cities uncover hundreds of skeletons, piled deep. These are often the remains of people who died horribly in the Black Death (1348–50) or in the later plagues that raged through Asia and Europe. The bodies were thrown into open pits and covered in quicklime to make them decompose quickly. They were then hastily covered with soil.

SPOOKED OUT

Monsters, vampires, skeletons and devils make fun costumes at Halloween, but at one time masks and costumes really were designed to scare the living daylights out of anyone who saw them.

MASKS AND MAGIC

Africa is famous for its masks, made to be worn in dances, entertainments, funerals or secret ceremonies. Some were masks of animals or people, some of spirits or ghosts. All were believed to have magical powers. Some masks were beautiful, but others were hideous, designed to chill the blood and horrify.

WITCH DOCTORS

Before medicines became widely available, many cultures around the world had witch doctors. It was believed that these wise men or women could interact with the spirit world to protect people from witchcraft. They also used herbal medicine to assist with childbirth, tooth extraction and illness. If their remedies failed, they commonly blamed the failure on the displeasure of the gods.

DAY OF THE DEAD

Dressed-up skeleton dolls, skull-shaped sweets, parades of revelers in skeleton costumes – welcome to Mexico's Day of the Dead, celebrated each year at the beginning of November. Morbid and miserable? Not at all! This ancient festival is all about honoring and celebrating the lives of the dead. Deceased children are remembered on 1st November (All Saints Day), and adults on 2nd November (All Souls Day).

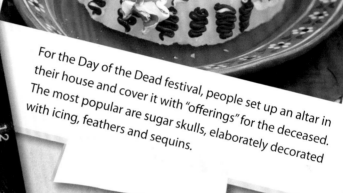

For the Day of the Dead festival, people set up an altar in their house and cover it with "offerings" for the deceased. The most popular are sugar skulls, elaborately decorated with icing, feathers and sequins.

DID YOU KNOW?

HEAD SHRINKERS

Long ago, the Shuar and Achuar warriors of the South American rain forest would cut off the heads of their enemies. They removed the skull and brain, boiled the remains, cut away the flesh and dried the skin with hot sand. Why did they shrink the heads? To win control of the dead man's spirit. Sometimes the heads were worn on cords around the neck.

AMAZING!

DEVIL MASKS

For Fastnacht, a carnival held before Lent in southern Germany, Switzerland and Austria, people wear scary carnival masks that look like devils with twisted faces. These represent the dark spirits of winter, which must be hunted down and expelled before Spring can come and life can start over again.

BEASTLY BEAUTY

People will go to extraordinary lengths to "look good." Over the ages, they have done some gruesome things to themselves in the name of beauty.

BIG WIGS

In the 1770s, the most fashionable ladies of Paris and London wore towering wigs and hairpieces. These were built around horsehair pads and were held together with pins, wire, ribbons, powder and a kind of grease called pomade. If the wigs weren't looked after properly, they soon attracted vermin and even, so they say, nesting mice!

FAT AS THAT... OR THIN AS A PIN?

In the 1860s the beautiful wives of King Rumanika of Karagwe, in Africa, were forced to drink milk all day long until they became as fat as seals and could no longer stand upright. At much the same time in Europe, incredibly narrow waists were in fashion. Ladies wore corsets that were laced so tightly that they deformed the body and damaged the ribs, heart and lungs.

LIQUID FAT

Today, over 400,000 people a year in the United States have liposuction to remove bulges from their bodies and re-shape themselves. A tube is inserted under the skin – most commonly on the thighs, buttocks, neck, upper arms and calves – and the fat there is broken down and sucked out by the jugful – how gross!

DID YOU KNOW?

GRUESOME GAP-FILLERS

False teeth were originally made from second-hand human or animal teeth. US President George Washington's fine set of false choppers was made out of hippopotamus tusk!

BAD MAKE-UP DAY

In the days of the Roman Empire, a woman might use cosmetics made of onions in chicken fat, crushed beetles, animal urine, soot, vinegar, asses' milk, sulfur, or as a very special treat, expensively imported crocodile dung. So what is in modern make-up? You'll need an advanced knowledge of chemistry to understand the ingredients!

TOOTH WHITENERS

People have always wanted gleaming teeth. Before good dentists came along, all sorts of toothpastes and mouthwashes were invented, and some of them were pretty gruesome! How would you fancy brushing with tortoise blood, burnt mouse heads, stale urine, charcoal or cuttlefish bone?

EXTREME BODIES

Huge lip plates, painted skin, body piercings and neck rings – humans have deformed and mistreated their bodies in the strangest ways over the ages.

BODY PIERCING

For more than 5,000 years, people have been piercing their bodies. Sometimes they do it for religious reasons, but often it's just a form of self-expression. A few people go wild and have hundreds, or even thousands, of piercings – the world record holder claimed, in 2012, to have 9,000!

NICE PLATE!

The Mursi or Mun people live in an isolated part of southwestern Ethiopia, in Africa. Traditionally, they paint their bodies with sacred clays, and the women wear large clay "plates" in their lower lips, used to serve food to their husband. Increasingly, the plates are also worn as a way of earning extra money from tourists.

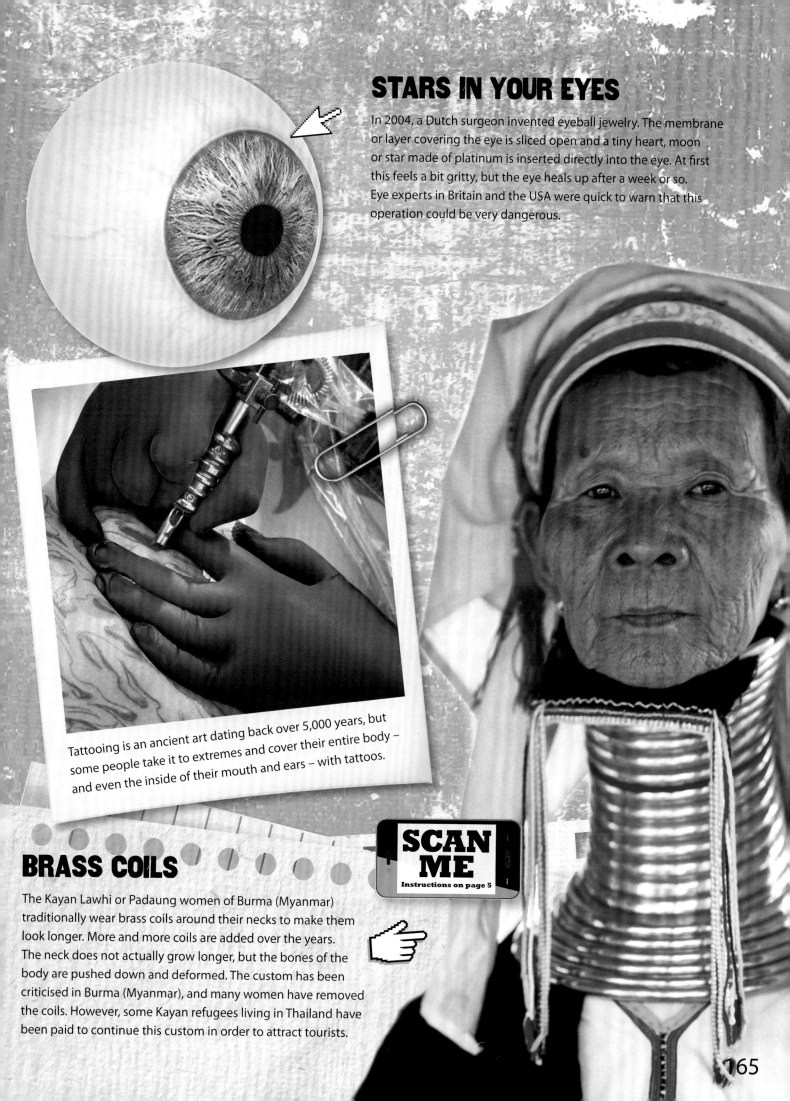

STARS IN YOUR EYES

In 2004, a Dutch surgeon invented eyeball jewelry. The membrane or layer covering the eye is sliced open and a tiny heart, moon or star made of platinum is inserted directly into the eye. At first this feels a bit gritty, but the eye heals up after a week or so. Eye experts in Britain and the USA were quick to warn that this operation could be very dangerous.

Tattooing is an ancient art dating back over 5,000 years, but some people take it to extremes and cover their entire body – and even the inside of their mouth and ears – with tattoos.

SCAN ME
Instructions on page 5

BRASS COILS

The Kayan Lawhi or Padaung women of Burma (Myanmar) traditionally wear brass coils around their necks to make them look longer. More and more coils are added over the years. The neck does not actually grow longer, but the bones of the body are pushed down and deformed. The custom has been criticised in Burma (Myanmar), and many women have removed the coils. However, some Kayan refugees living in Thailand have been paid to continue this custom in order to attract tourists.

FREAKY FOODS

We think animals have gross eating habits, but when it comes to freaky food, we humans take the maggot-filled biscuit! Take a look at some of the rotten, wriggling and rank foods that people eat – you'll be amazed!

CRUNCH TIME!

It's a mystery why anyone would want to eat a cockroach. These insects carry nasty diseases, and they smell really bad! In 2012, a man died after eating dozens of cockroaches in a pet shop bug-eating competition. He choked to death on the legs and crunchy skin.

HANDY AND HEALTHY

People eat what they can find, grow or buy, and if there are lots of grubs around – well, you eat grubs. They are easy to find and catch, and each one is a mouthful of good-quality protein, and is low in fat. That makes them both handy and healthy!

TASTY TARANTULAS

If you were offered a plate of crispy spiders, would you be willing to try one? These deep-fried tarantulas are a delicacy in Cambodia, Southeast Asia. They are fried until the legs turn crunchy, and the insides are soft but not runny!

DID YOU KNOW?

YOU ARE WHAT YOU EAT

When you eat, your body turns food into energy, muscles, fat and other important body bits. If you eat strange things, you may get some odd changes to your body. Eating beetroot turns your wee pink, while eating asparagus can give it a peculiar whiff. Athletes can grow more muscle by eating kangaroos rather than pigs. If you eat the wrong stuff, you could get ill – some parts of a puffer fish contain a deadly poison.

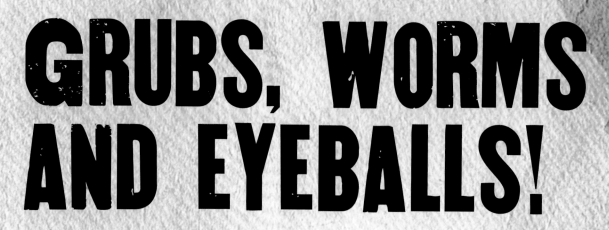

GRUBS, WORMS AND EYEBALLS!

These bizarre tidbits may look disgusting to you, but to someone else they are tasty treats, packed with goodness, and delicious too!

TUCK IN!

People in Southeast Asia don't let any food go to waste – that's why food stalls often sell a delicious chicken or duck combo kebab of roasted hearts, feet and tails. Chicken gizzards (stomachs) are a popular traditional food in China.

GOURMET GRUBS

They are large, squashy, juicy, tasty and really good for you – so why not tuck into a nice fat grub? Witchetty grubs come from Australia and are the larvae (caterpillars) of moths. They taste a bit like scrambled eggs and can be eaten raw or lightly cooked.

SCAN ME
Instructions on page 5

SWEET SNACK

Silk worms are the larvae of moths, and they are used to make silk. In Burma (Myanmar), they are deep-fried until they puff up like corn snacks, and are served with a lovely coating of honey.

DID YOU KNOW?

FRUIT BAT SOUP

In the islands around Thailand, a whole fruit bat is dunked live into a simmering pot to make a popular soup. Herbs, spices and coconut milk are added, but they can't take away the nasty taste of bat. These flying mammals also carry diseases, so this is not a recipe we recommend!

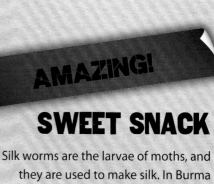

If someone offers you a sheep's eye, remember to pop it into your mouth whole. Then crunch it up to enjoy the slimy liquid pouring out – it's a delicacy in parts of Arabia and Africa.

FREAKY FOOD HERO

William Buckland (1784–1856) was a freaky food hero. His ambition was to eat an example of every animal that lived, from puppies to panthers. He even tried bats' wee. His favorite dish was mice on toast, but he wasn't keen on insects, especially bluebottles and earwigs.

You can eat mealworms (baby beetles) raw, but the best way is to dry roast them, just like peanuts. Then you can add them to muffins – yum!

MORE FREAKY FOODS

If you like trying new foods, you need to travel. These dishes are national favorites around the world.

HOPPY MEAL

There are millions more kangaroos in Australia than there are humans. In fact, there are so many roos jumping about that eating them is one way to control their numbers. Kangaroo meat is also very healthy, because it's packed with protein and has less fat than other meats.

PIG TAILS

The French are famous for their wonderful cooking skills, so it's no wonder they can make pigs' heads and tails taste good. The tails need to be cooked slowly to get the best flavor, but nibbling on the skinny, bony bits is still hard work, and not as good as barbecue spare ribs!

ANT CROUTONS

Ants are added to salads in Venezuela. They are deep-fried and then sprinkled over the top to add a slightly smoky flavor and a crunch!

AMAZING!

FURRY FRIENDS

We think of guinea-pigs as pets, but in Peru people think of these little furry animals as… lunch! They are bred on guinea-pig farms. People often cook them over an open flame and serve them up on a bed of lettuce.

Horsemeat is often used in Switzerland to make horseburgers and casseroles. It tastes so similar to beef that it can be difficult to tell the difference.

TERMITE TREAT

Children in Uganda can't get their hands on sweets and chocolate very easily, but they can enjoy a healthier treat – termites! These ant-like insects are caught in their flying season. Their wings are removed and then they are boiled and fried.

WOULD YOU EAT THIS?

Do you believe that a dog is man's best friend? Or do you think there's nothing better than dog stew? What's taboo (not acceptable) in one country may be perfectly alright somewhere else!

BARKING MAD

In Hawaii, puppies are cooked over a bed of burning coals and served with a dish of sweet potatoes. Long ago, Mexican hairless dogs were bred to be eaten, and were the Aztecs' main meat. Dogs have been eaten in Korea for more than 6,000 years, and dog dishes are still popular there today.

ANYONE FOR UDDER?

Udders are the part of a cow where milk is made, and where calves suck to get at the milk. It's hard to believe, but for centuries they were a popular type of meat in England and France. Udders were boiled and added to stews, or cooked and sliced as cold meat, like ham.

GOAT BURGER

Hot, dry countries are not always the best place to rear cattle, which need lots of green grass to thrive. Instead, people rear goats and turn their meat into burgers, pies or stews. Donkeys, mules and water buffalo are also likely to be on the menu.

A single swarm of locusts can contain many millions of flying insects, and as they travel they eat every plant in their path. What better way to get your own back than to tuck into a plateful of boiled locusts?

WARNING!

CHOKING HAZARD

If you fancy eating grasshoppers or locusts, it's a good idea to remove their long, spindly hind legs first. Although the legs have got some delicious meat in them, they are also covered in small spines, and can get caught in your throat, just like fish bones.

FRIED FEET

Bears used to live in the forests of Europe, and were often hunted for food. A favorite treat in several countries was a dish of bears' paws. They were coated in breadcrumbs and fried in butter or oil, just like chicken nuggets!

12

BLOOD SAUSAGE, BRAINS AND OTHER GRUESOME FOODS

Would you eat something if you could see its face looking back at you? Eating heads and brains is weird!

HEAD CHEESE

Head cheese isn't made of cheese, but the bad news is that it's definitely made of heads! Usually pigs' or calves' heads are used. Chefs are told to remove the eyes and skin, and to clear the ear canals of wax – how gross! The meat is then boiled, and a pig's foot may be added for more flavor.

HEADS UP

If you had to cook a calf's head (a popular dish in France known as *tête de veau*), where would you begin? You'd remove all the fur and skin first. Next, you'd cut it in half, roll it around a calf's tongue and cook it in a big pan with water and seasoning for about five hours. Now serve it cut into slices, with a bit of brain on top – how gross is that?

Blood sausages are popular around the world, and in England they are part of a fried breakfast. They are called black pudding, and are made from pigs' blood.

MIND OVER MATTER

Brains are soft, squishy and spongy, so eating them is more like eating a grainy jelly than eating other types of meat. They are enjoyed all over the world, and are served in many different ways, from boiling to frying. In some places, brains are spread on toast with salt, and in Austria pig brains are cooked into scrambled egg.

FAT FURTERS

Lots of people love to eat the pale pink sausages called frankfurters – but would you still eat one if you knew what went into it? Cheap frankfurters are made from a meat paste made in a factory from leftover bits of pig. The paste is then mashed with fake flavors and colors, and extra water and salt are added.

HAVE SOME MORE?

Are you someone who's always ready for second helpings? You might not be so keen on some of these lovely dishes!

SLIMY STARTERS

Collecting and selling Mopani worms is big business in southern Africa. These grubs are caterpillars that live on trees, and they are served up in homes and restaurants. Before they are eaten, the caterpillars are squeezed until their green, slimy insides slide out!

DEAD AND RED

Did you know that some red food dye, such as the kind used to color icing, gets its color from dead insects called cochineals? They live on cactuses and have to be collected by hand to be turned into a natural dye. Cochineal coloring is also added to meats to make them look fresh.

COFFEE SURPRISE

You could finish your gruesome meal with a delightful cup of kopi luwak coffee. It is made from coffee beans that have been eaten and pooed out by wild civets (cat-like animals). It has a slight taste of chocolate…

This is probably the most disgusting cheese in the world! It is called *casu marzu*, and is full of wriggling, munching maggots that break down the cheese's fats.

DID YOU KNOW?

KILLER BEANS

Dried kidney beans look harmless, but they can make you extremely ill if they are not properly prepared. The beans make a poison to stop insects from eating them, but it can make humans sick, too. The poison can be destroyed by soaking the beans for 12 hours and then cooking them. Luckily, canned kidney beans are completely safe.

MEDICAL MATTERS

The history of medicine reveals some gruesome complaints and ghastly treatments, as well as weird and wacky ways of dealing with bodies – both alive and dead.

AMAZING!

PAINFUL PAST

We are lucky to live in the modern age of scientific medicine, with antibiotics and anesthetics readily available. Not that long ago, surgeons sawed off arms and legs without painkillers.

SWALLOWED!

People have been known to swallow all kinds of strange things. One woman in Canada in the 1920s swallowed more than 2,500 objects, including almost 1,000 bent pins! Other things found inside us include metal screws, buttons, safety pins, a toy dog, stones, keys and even a fork!

CORPSES

Long ago, people happily passed by corpses rotting on gibbets, but thought it wrong to dissect (cut up) bodies to see how they worked. However, doctors needed to know, and some were prepared to pay thieves to dig up newly buried bodies from graveyards so they could practice on them.

GRUESOME DISEASES

Many killer-diseases, such as smallpox, have been conquered by medical science, but new bugs and epidemics remain a global threat. Some grisly conditions that people have had to endure include acromegaly – a disease that turns people into hulking giants; leprosy, which causes noses, fingers and toes to drop off; and flesh-eating disease, in which skin tissue is hideously destroyed by bacteria.

11A ▶

12

11A ▶

12

PRESERVING BODIES

Left alone, a dead body decomposes or rots, but there are a number of ways to preserve bodies.

HOLY RELICS

In the Middle Ages, churches and kings kept bones, skulls, fingers and other body parts of saints as holy relics. King Louis IX (St Louis) of France collected all kinds of Christian relics. When, in 1270, he died in North Africa, his own bones were boiled until all the flesh was gone, so they could be taken back to France.

AMAZING!

PICKLED IN BRANDY

Admiral Nelson's victory at the Battle of Trafalgar, in 1805, was met with celebration and sadness – the threat to England of invasion by Napoleon had been removed, but Nelson was dead. On board ship, his body was placed in a large barrel filled with brandy to preserve it, while it was sailed back to England. It was then put in a brandy-filled lead coffin while the state funeral was arranged. Alcohol preserved his body for over two months (October 21, 1805, to January 9, 1806).

Suicide was often a ritual, performed in a special way. To avoid dishonor, a Japanese nobleman would slash his stomach open with his samurai sword.

EMBALMING

Undertakers embalm bodies for funerals, replacing blood in the veins with chemicals. They make the body look as lifelike as possible, even sewing up the lips to keep the mouth shut. Sometimes embalmed bodies are put on public display. The North Korean leader Kim Il Sung (d. 1994) lies in a glass case inside a palace.

RIGOR MORTIS

Rigor mortis is the stiffening of a body after death. It starts 3 to 4 hours after a person has died. Within 12 hours a body may be completely rigid, although it stiffens more quickly in a warm room. Rigor wears off within 2 to 2½ days.

MODERN MUMMIFICATION

Long ago, the Egyptians mummified bodies to preserve them. They removed the insides, sucking out the brain through the nose, then dried and padded the corpse, and wrapped it in cloth. Today, a different method is used. Bodies (including those of pet cats) are submerged in preservation fluid for several months. It's claimed that this way the body's DNA is preserved, so the individual could one day be cloned back to life.

BODY WORLDS

The first anatomists had to work fast to dissect bodies before they decomposed. Now, science has found ways to keep bodies lifelike forever.

BOTTLED!

From the late 1800s, scientists used chemicals such as formaldehyde to kill bacteria and preserve human and animal remains. Museums kept pickled fish, reptiles and other animals, while medical schools kept human body parts. Although formaldehyde slows down decay, it cannot preserve a body forever.

PLASTIC PEOPLE

Plastination is a technique invented in the 1970s by German anatomist Gunther von Hagens. Basically he invented a way to make long-lasting plastic bodies. Plastination works by replacing water and fat in a dead body with plastics called polymer resins. The plastics preserve the body so that it does not smell, and can be handled by students or posed to look lifelike.

182

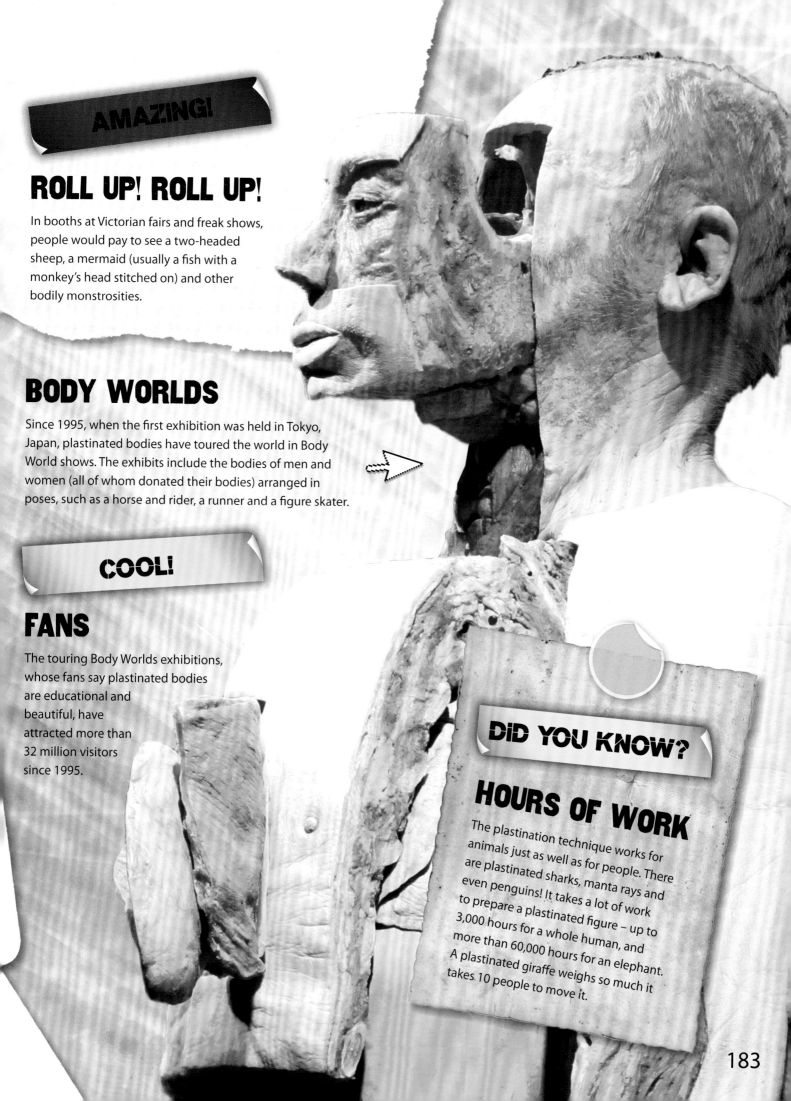

ROLL UP! ROLL UP!

In booths at Victorian fairs and freak shows, people would pay to see a two-headed sheep, a mermaid (usually a fish with a monkey's head stitched on) and other bodily monstrosities.

BODY WORLDS

Since 1995, when the first exhibition was held in Tokyo, Japan, plastinated bodies have toured the world in Body World shows. The exhibits include the bodies of men and women (all of whom donated their bodies) arranged in poses, such as a horse and rider, a runner and a figure skater.

COOL!

FANS

The touring Body Worlds exhibitions, whose fans say plastinated bodies are educational and beautiful, have attracted more than 32 million visitors since 1995.

DID YOU KNOW?

HOURS OF WORK

The plastination technique works for animals just as well as for people. There are plastinated sharks, manta rays and even penguins! It takes a lot of work to prepare a plastinated figure – up to 3,000 hours for a whole human, and more than 60,000 hours for an elephant. A plastinated giraffe weighs so much it takes 10 people to move it.

PAIN AND MORE PAIN

Until the 1800s, surgery was painful and dangerous. There were no painkillers or drugs, and there was lots of dirt and infection!

BLIND EGYPTIANS!

Curious cures were common in ancient times. To treat blindness, ancient Egyptians mashed up pigs' eyes, added honey and red ocher (an earthy pigment containing ferric oxide), and then poured the mixture into the patient's ear!

HOLE IN THE HEAD

Since ancient Egyptian times, people have had holes drilled through their skulls to relieve pressure beneath the bone. Called trepanning, this treatment was believed to cure fits and madness. The ancient Egyptians did it without anesthetics – yikes!

Wounded from the Crimean War (1850s) ended up in filthy hospitals full of rats – until nurse Florence Nightingale came along and revolutionized nursing.

OPEN WIDE

From the Middle Ages to the 19th century, having a tooth out meant letting a barber yank away with pliers – and no anesthetic. From the 18th century, people took laudanum to ease the pain. It contained opium, which turned some people into drug addicts.

11A

12

11A

GANGRENE OR MAGGOTS?

Gangrene is an infection in an unclean wound that eats away tissue. What might start as an infected toe could lead to a rotting leg, and then amputation – and possibly death. In the past, one remedy was maggots! Applied to the wound, the maggots munched away at the dead flesh, giving the patient a chance of recovery.

WARNING!

PHEW!

Gangrenous wounds swell up, smell foul and weep pus, and the skin turns from red, to brown, to black.

SURGERY AT SEA

In the days of sail, wounded sailors went "under the knife" while the ship tossed on the waves. The surgeon strapped his patient to a table, took seconds to cut off an arm or leg, slapped on hot tar to seal the wound, then moved on to the next man. Many patients died of shock, or infection from dirty knives and saws.

185

BODY SNATCHERS

Doctors learn about the body by cutting it open. But for many years, practical anatomy was against the law. To get a body, a doctor had to pay a body snatcher.

DID YOU KNOW?

AGAINST THE LAW

Throughout Medieval Europe and the early Renaissance, the Catholic Church prohibited the mutilation (cutting up) of Christian bodies, and civil laws forbade the dissection of corpses in general.

RAISING THE DEAD

Before 1832, when a law was passed allowing more bodies to be used for medical dissection, only the corpses of hanged murderers were available to medical students. Sometimes doctors turned to grave robbers – known as "resurrection men" because they "raised the dead" – to supply them with bodies.

SCALPELS OUT

Andreas Vesalius (1514–64) revolutionized the study of human anatomy. He broke with Medieval tradition by personally cutting up corpses (executed criminals) in front of his students, and challenging the centuries-old teachings of Galen that were normally taught to anatomy students. At Padua University, his students had to work in secret, in rooms with no windows, so the smell wouldn't alert the authorities. During the 17th century, the public would sometimes pay to watch anatomy lessons, as here at the University of Leiden, Holland.

MORTSAFES

Rich families locked up their dead inside stone vaults, which were fairly secure. Ordinary graves were more at risk from theft. From 1816, people could buy an iron grid or box, called a "mortsafe," to put over a grave, so that robbers couldn't force off the gravestone and steal the body inside.

BURKE AND HARE

In Scotland, in the early 1800s, two body snatchers named William Burke and William Hare sold corpses to an Edinburgh doctor, Robert Knox. When demand exceeded supply, the pair turned to murder, and killed 16 people. Later, Hare put the blame on Burke, who was hanged in 1829. The expression "to burke" meant to strangle someone, leaving no sign of violence.

TUNNEL ROBBERS

To guard against body-theft, which became increasingly common, cemetery guardians were posted to keep watch from specially built towers. Some grave robbers dug tunnels to get into graves, looping a rope around the corpse to pull it out.

BEAUTY TREATMENTS

In pursuit of beauty, people don't always stop to consider the medical consequences. Beauty treatments can be painful, and even fatal.

PLUCK IT OUT

In Europe in the 1400s to 1500s, fashion-conscious women plucked not only their eyebrows, but also all the hair from the front of their heads. The idea was to make the hairline recede and the forehead look bigger – ouch!

Plunging your feet into a fish spa bath feels pretty weird. As the "doctor fish" nibble away at the feet looking for food, they dislodge little bits of old, dead skin. Some US states have banned fish spas, fearing they could spread infections.

THE BIG SQUEEZE

One way that many people tackle obesity is to have a gastric band fitted to their stomach to slow down eating and reduce their appetite. Although often successful, complications can occur. The band can slip, bulge through the skin, or cause blood clots. Successful weight loss also leaves a person with baggy sacs of loose, wrinkly skin – lovely!

WHITE FOR DANGER

In Japan, a geisha girl's idea of beauty was to have porcelain-white skin, which she got by applying a lead-based paste to her face and neck. The white lead was highly toxic, and led to illness and an early death for some geishas.

FAT HOOVER

Liposuction to remove fat is in great demand, but things can go dreadfully wrong. Small pieces of fat can pass into the bloodstream and cause blockages. This is the most common cause of death following liposuction.

BOTOX

For a face free of wrinkles, people inject botox protein, made from botulinum toxin – a deadly poison! In tiny amounts, botox gets rid of wrinkles by paralyzing the muscles that cause them. But it can also cause botulism, a serious and life-threatening illness.

GHOULISH MONSTERS

Myths are ancient tales of gods and goddesses, heroes, demons and monsters. They reflect our deepest feelings, from love and happiness to terror, savagery and fear of death.

HELPLESS HUMANS

Modern film-makers love to scare us with the idea that science-fiction monsters, such as androids or cyborgs, might one day turn on humans and take over the world. Androids are robots with a human-like appearance, and cyborgs are beings with both living and robotic parts, such as Darth Vada from the *Star Wars* movies.

OUR VIVID IMAGINATION

The human imagination feeds on fear. In the shadows and darkness, we may picture devils and demons, blood-drinking vampires, shambling graveyard zombies, howling werewolves or headless ghosts. Bats, giant spiders, snakes and toads may be seen as agents of evil or witchcraft. Dogs with burning eyes or blood-curdling banshees may be messengers of death.

Since the earliest days of storytelling, death has been personified as a figure or fictional character. In western culture, he is usually pictured as a skeleton. Sometimes death is portrayed as Azrael, the angel of death. Father Time is also sometimes said to be death.

LOVE OF HORROR

We may be less superstitious and more scientific than our ancestors, but the popularity of movies, books and computer games that are dedicated to sheer horror shows that these bad dreams still linger. People in the 21st century seem to enjoy being terrified every bit as much as people in ancient Greece or Rome – so let's bring on the shivers!

11A ► 12

MYTHOLOGICAL MONSTERS

The myths of ancient Greece and Rome are the stuff of nightmares. They tell of terrifying monsters and vengeful gods.

THREE HEADS

Beware the jaws of Cerberus, the hound of hell who guarded the gates of the Underworld, home to the dead. With his three heads, he could see the past, present and future. Cerberus snarled, slavered and slobbered, and had a taste for living flesh. He only allowed in the souls of the dead – and made sure that none of these ever left.

DON'T LOOK NOW!

Medusa was a monster – a Gorgon with a writhing tangle of hissing snakes in place of hair. Anyone who looked into her eyes was turned to stone. She was beheaded by the hero Perseus, who then used her head as a weapon.

AMAZING!

DODGY DNA

Cerberus's mother was Echidna, who was half snake and half woman. His father was Typhon, a terrifying giant who breathed fire.

HORRID HARPIES

The Harpies were winged creatures, sometimes shown as terrible hags with wings and talons. They snatched food, spread filth and caused famine.

THE MINOTAUR

On the island of Crete there was a maze called the Labyrinth. Trapped at its heart was a bellowing, raging monster – half man and half bull – called the Minotaur. Every seven years this beast ate seven youths and seven maidens, specially sent from Athens. It was slain by a hero named Theseus.

SIREN SONGS

The Sirens were water nymphs. Passing sailors who heard their sweet song became drowsy and dreamy, and were unaware that they were being lured to a terrible death.

MAN-EATER

The Cyclopes were gruesome, one-eyed giants armed with clubs. The most famous was Polyphemus, who captured the Greek hero Odysseus and his friends and trapped them in his cave. Odysseus attacked and blinded the giant, plunging a burning stake into his one eye.

DRACULA AND FRANKENSTEIN

Vampires and crazed monsters are the subject of many folk tales, superstitions and legends, and have fueled the imagination of writers and film makers.

BLOOD-SUCKERS

A belief in vampires was common in the 1700s and 1800s, especially in regions of southeastern Europe, such as Transylvania, in Romania. Country folk claimed that vampires really existed, and that these "un-dead" sucked the blood from animals and humans with their fangs. Anyone bitten by a vampire would become one themselves.

FRANKENSTEIN'S MONSTER

Frankenstein was one of the first-ever science fiction novels. Written in 1818 by English author Mary Shelley, it tells the story of a student, Victor Frankenstein, who creates a living being from bits of corpses, and brings it to life. The creature is treated very unkindly by humans, and seeks furious revenge on its maker. Recreated in countless theater, film and television adaptations, this story has been giving people the shivers ever since.

GOTHIC HORROR

In many modern film and television tales of vampires, we see a coffin lid creak open deep in a burial vault in some ruined castle. Out of it steps a pale figure in a billowing black cloak. This person sets out into the night with a deadly mission – to fasten their teeth into the throat of an innocent victim, until bloated with blood. Such tales are mostly based on the gothic novel *Dracula*, written by the Irish novelist, Bram Stoker, in 1897.

COOL FACT!

FIT FOR VAMPIRES

The name Dracula was taken from the Draculesti – the princes of Wallachia, Romania, in the 1400s. One of them, Vlad III, impaled thousands of his enemies on wooden stakes. Bran Castle, situated on the border between Transylvania and Wallachia, is one of several castles claiming links with the Dracula story.

KEEP OFF!

It was believed that the only things that would keep vampires at bay were garlands of garlic or Christian crucifixes. And the only way to kill a vampire? A stake driven through the heart while the vampire slept.

ZOMBIES AND WEREWOLVES

Creatures of the night, rotting corpses brought back to life, bloodthirsty shape-shifters... The worst fears of our ancestors are kept alive in modern horror movies.

WEREWOLVES

Fear of werewolves dates back to Greek and Roman times, and was common in Europe during the Middle Ages. A werewolf was a person who could turn him or herself into a huge wolf and then turn back into their human form. As a wolf, the creature was said to hunt children, raid graveyards and behave in a terrifying and destructive manner.

GHASTLY GHOULS

The word "ghoul" comes from the Arabic for "seizer" or "demon." Originally, ghouls were believed to be evil spirits that lurked in the desert. They could take on the shape of hyenas, seizing and attacking travelers and then crunching up their bodies and bones. Sometimes they would take on the shape of the person they had just eaten.

ZOMBIES

Followers of the West African religion known as vodun or voodoo believe that sorcerers can bring dead people back to life and keep them under their control. Meet the "un-dead," or "zombies." Such beliefs passed from Africa to the Caribbean, especially to Haiti. The Haitian lord of death is known as Baron Samedi. Only his magic can stop dead bodies being turned into zombies. Mass zombie horror has become a feature of many modern movies and cults.

SPIRITS OF EVIL

In the days when people believed in witches, they also believed in "familiar spirits." These were agents of the Devil, who helped the witches do evil. They might take the form of demons, toads, crows, hares or black cats.

Haiti's lord of death, Baron Samedi, is often shown as a scary skeleton wearing a top hat.

DiD YOU KNOW?

HOWLING AT THE MOON

In many modern werewolf tales, when the werewolf turns into their wolf form, they can be heard howling eerily at the full moon. Real wolves are often more active on bright, clear nights, which is probably where the idea of howling at the moon came from. In modern tales and horror films, a werewolf can only be killed with a silver bullet.

MESSENGERS OF DEATH

Sometimes people believe they have been warned – by a spirit or messenger of death – that they will soon die. That's enough to make your blood run cold!

WAIL OF THE BANSHEE

A banshee is a female spirit of the Celtic lands, who signals the approach of death with an unearthly wail that rises and falls in the night. Sometimes she may be seen washing bloodstained clothes. The banshee is regarded as one of the fairy folk, but may also be linked to ancient beliefs in the Morrigan, an Irish goddess who flies over warriors slaughtered in battle, in the form of a crow.

If you see your double (in German, your *Doppelgänger*) walking toward you, watch out! Some say this is an omen of your own death!

YAMA

In the Hindu religion, Yama is the much-feared god of death. Nobody can stop him coming, or change the timing of his visit. His two dogs, each with four eyes and wide nostrils, guard the road to his abode.

HOUNDS OF HELL

Imagine a ghostly dog with a hairy black coat and burning red eyes, prowling through the night and howling, before vanishing into the shadows. According to the folklore of many lands, just a glimpse of this hell-hound can be a warning of death to come.

11A ▶

12

11A ▶

AMAZING!

DANCE OF DEATH

In the Middle Ages, many pictures show Death leading his victims away from the living world in a "dance of death." Nobody can escape his bony grasp – young or old, rich or poor.

THE GRIM REAPER

From the 15th century onward, the figure of Death was shown as a skeleton wrapped in a black, hooded robe. Often his face could not be seen. He carried a scythe, to show that his job was to cut the ties between a person's soul and their body. Sometimes he was also shown carrying an hourglass, to show that a person's time on Earth had run out.

DEADLY DISASTERS

Plagues, famine, fires and floods leave gruesome scenes of devastation in their wake. When a terrible tragedy occurs, it shocks us to the core.

CRASH SCENE

Disasters of our own making, such as a car, train or airplane crash, are just as horrific as natural disasters. Whether they are the result of human error or mechanical failure, the consequences are equally gruesome. We also have the added burden of guilt, because someone, somewhere, was responsible, and maybe the disaster could have been avoided.

NATURE UNTAMED

Real-life horror stories are often about losing control. Human beings may be brave and clever, but they are helpless when pitted against the untamed forces of nature. In a great earthquake or a sudden flood, we may not stand a chance, with nowhere left to run or hide.

Luckily the human body has a crisis default. Adrenaline is the chemical with superpowers that kicks in when we are scared. It helps us to run away from danger, but it also gives us the energy to make extreme efforts – to rescue other people, to struggle against the odds and even to save lives.

WARNING!

ATOM BOMB

Very occasionally, we deliberately cause unspeakable damage on a scale equal to a major natural disaster. Atomic bombs have enough destructive power to wipe out an entire city in an instant. In 1945, the United States dropped atomic bombs on the Japanese cities of Hiroshima and Nagasaki. Up to 166,000 people in Hiroshima and 80,000 in Nagasaki died from falling debris, radiation sickness or burns.

QUAKES AND WAVES

Is the ground beneath us solid and safe? No! The planet's crust quakes and shakes. Earthquakes can destroy great cities, and also trigger terrifying walls of water, called tsunamis.

WHY THE BIG SHAKE UP?

The rocks that make up the Earth's surface are a bit like an eggshell cracked into about 20 sections, called plates. These float on a layer of gooey rock, called mantle. The edges of the plates often bump, grind and crunch together, with a force powerful enough to push up the world's biggest mountain ranges.

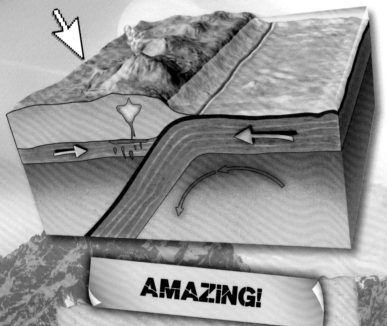

TERROR QUAKES

Just before an earthquake happens, the world suddenly falls silent. Even the dogs stop barking. Suddenly there is a great rumble or roar. Highways crack open, bridges fall into rivers and apartment blocks collapse into rubble. Homes are crushed like cardboard. Gas pipes catch fire and water mains burst open. Such is the terror of a major earthquake.

AMAZING!

WORST EVER

The 1556 earthquake in Shaanxi, China, had the worst death toll of any earthquake in history – it killed about 830,000 people.

BIGGEST EVER

The biggest-ever earthquake struck Valdivia, Chile, in 1960, with a magnitude of 9.5.

WALLS OF WATER

An earthquake below the ocean floor can trigger a massive shock. The pressure sends a mighty whoosh of water racing through the ocean. As it approaches the coast, this is raised into a giant wave. The sea drains back from beaches, and then a wall of water rushes in. The Japanese tsunami of 2011 towered to a height of 40.4 m (133 ft) and in places smashed its way 6 miles (10 km) inland. It killed 15,883 people and caused disastrous accidents at nuclear power plants.

SCAN ME
Instructions on page 5

HAITI'S HORROR

When a magnitude 7.0 earthquake struck Haiti in 2010, its people lost everything. At least 220,000 people were killed, over 300,000 were injured and 1.5 million were made homeless. More than 293,000 houses and 4,000 schools were badly damaged or destroyed, and the capital, Port-au-Prince, was engulfed in tonnes of rubble.

TSUNAMI HAZARD ZONE

IN CASE OF EARTHQUAKE GO TO HIGH GROUND OR INLAND

VOLCANO!

Long ago, people thought that the sulfurous, glowing craters of volcanoes were the gateways to hell. We still fear these mountains of fire today – with good reason!

TEMPTING FATE

The green slopes of a tropical volcano might seem to be the ideal place to start a farm. The soil is black, crumbly and very fertile. And who knows, the volcano might not erupt for hundreds of years. But what if you are unlucky? When a volcano blows its top, it can rip the whole mountainside apart. You may be poisoned by deadly gas, bombed by rocks, choked by ash, swallowed up by molten rock or burnt alive!

RING OF FIRE

The rim of the Pacific Ocean is often called the Ring of Fire. The geology there is restless along a vast arc that takes in New Zealand, Southeast Asia, Japan, Russia and North and South America. This "ring" has 452 volcanoes, and a high risk of spectacular earthquakes and tsunamis. Welcome to the ultimate danger zone!

BURIED ALIVE

When Italy's Mount Vesuvius erupted in 79 AD, the port of Herculaneum was engulfed by a torrent of boiling mud 13 m (42 ft) deep. Archeologists have found the skeletons of victims who were trying to escape by boat. The inland town of Pompeii was buried under ash, in places 3.5 m (11.5 ft) deep. Where corpses were buried, their bodies left cavities in the ash. By filling these spaces with plaster, archeologists have been able to recreate the likeness of the victims at the moment they died.

COOL FACT!

BIG BANG

The 1883 explosion of Krakatoa, a volcanic island in Indonesia, is said to have been heard about 3,000 miles (4,800 km) away. The eruption spewed ash 50 miles (80 km) into space. The death toll was somewhere between 36,000 and 120,000.

LAVA

Under the Earth's crust, Earth is made of hot, liquid rock, called magma. When this liquid rock erupts out of a volcano, it's called lava. The lava flows in red-hot rivers down the side of the volcano, and hardens as it cools. Cooled lava has formed many mountains and island chains.

ROLLING DEATH

A pyroclastic flow is a wall of smoke, gases and ash that can be as hot as 1,000°C (1,830°F). It can roll down a mountainside at over 155 mph (250 km/h). In 1902, a deadly pyroclastic flow from Mt Pelée in Martinique killed about 30,000 people in the town of Saint-Pierre.

HURRICANE WARNING

Hurricanes are also called typhoons, cyclones or tropical storms. Weather experts (Met officials) give them human names, such as Katrina, Fifi, Bob or Stan. This may sound more friendly, but don't be fooled – hurricanes spell disaster!

WHEEL OF WIND

Viewed from space, a hurricane looks like a vast wheel of thunder clouds and rain, churning around in a spiral as it sweeps across a warm ocean. At its center is a calmer area of low pressure, called the eye, but the winds circling that eye can be vicious. They can pile up gigantic waves and surges. These batter the coast and crash inland, causing flooding, mudslides, the destruction of property and loss of life.

AMAZING!

TEXAS TERROR

Probably the worst hurricane in US history hit the island city of Galveston, Texas, in 1900. It roared in at 145 mph (233 km/h), sending a storm surge over the island that destroyed thousands of homes and may have claimed about 8,000 lives.

GUST HORROR

The highest gust of wind ever recorded during a tropical storm was for Cyclone Olivia, which clocked up 253 mph (408 km/h) on Barrow Island, Australia in 1996.

HURRICANE HAVOC

Late summer and fall are the hurricane seasons in the United States. In August 2005, a hurricane named Katrina rampaged down the Gulf coast and hit the state of Louisiana full on. The wind howled and water surged inland. In New Orleans, bridges collapsed, and the levées (raised banks) protecting the city from floods failed and broke, pouring water into the streets. About 1,830 people died. The damage amounted to billions of dollars.

THE DEADLIEST EVER

The Bay of Bengal is known for brewing up devastating tropical storms, and the worst ever was the Bhola cyclone of 1970. This swept floods over the low-lying coast of Bangladesh and the delta lands of the Ganges river. About 500,000 people lost their lives, and in all about 3.6 million faced hardship. Villages, cattle and crops were destroyed.

TWISTERS

The sky is black with thunder clouds, but this is no normal storm. Snaking to the ground is a dark whirlwind, sweeping across the dusty plain. Nothing in the path of this tornado is safe – homes, schools, animals or humans.

FUNNELS OF FURY

Tornadoes take shape inside storm clouds. The winds that are created may spin around at speeds of about 110 mph (175 km/h). Sometimes they even exceed 300 mph (480 km/h). Soon, a dark funnel extends to the ground. This may be about 100 m (328 ft) wide, but a real monster may measure over 2 miles (3 km) across. The air pressure inside falls rapidly, sucking up dust and grit from the ground. The updraft can be severe, shattering houses and derailing trains.

AMAZING!

STORM CHASING

Most people have an instinctive reaction to a twister – run! It's best to head for a tornado shelter as quickly as possible. But others, called "storm chasers," prefer to follow twisters, to photograph them, record data or just thrill at the spectacle. It can be a dangerous and reckless game.

SCAN ME
Instructions on page 5

KILLER IN THE SKY

A tiger of a tornado ripped into Bangladesh in 1989. It trashed the cities of Daulatpur and Saturia, and probably killed about 1,300 people. About 12,000 were injured and about 80,000 were left homeless. Its trail of destruction was about 50 miles (80 km) long. This may have been the most damaging tornado in history.

FACT FILE

The famous Tri-State Tornado of 1925 devastated Missouri, Indiana and Illinois, killing 695 people.

Tornadoes have been known to rain down frogs and fishes that have been sucked up from ditches and ponds.

A tornado can lift a house off the ground and smash it into matchsticks. This house at Lapeer, Michigan, has had its side ripped off and is perched precariously.

Cold, dry air

Tornado Alley

Warm, dry air

Warm, moist air

TORNADO ALLEY

About 1,200 tornados strike the United States each year. The chief danger zone is the corridor of flat land between the Appalachian and Rocky Mountains, nicknamed Tornado Alley.

ROARING AVALANCHES

An avalanche gathers up snow, ice, soil, rocks and trees as it goes, until it weighs hundreds of thousands of tonnes. Anything in its path – people, houses, villages or vehicles – will be swept away. Better watch out!

WHITE DEATH

Snow can be wet, powdery, loose or closely packed. Any one of these can be fatal when hurtling down a mountain. An avalanche can be triggered naturally, when a mass of snow starts to break up during a thaw or storm, but skiing or using snowmobiles may also set one off.

BURIED ALIVE

If you are buried alive under an avalanche, you may have about 18 minutes to live before you suffocate. Your limbs may be broken, or you may die of hypothermia. The most important piece of equipment to carry is a beacon or transceiver, which sends out location signals to others on the mountain.

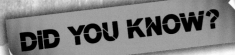
DID YOU KNOW?

"AVALANCHE!"

Sometimes mountain rangers set off avalanches on purpose, with explosives. These are controlled exercises to relieve the build-up of snow on the peak at a time when all is clear below.

SERIAL KILLER

Mount Huascarán in Peru is the world's cruelest mountain. In 1962, an avalanche of ice and rock buried whole towns and villages, killing 4,000 people. In 1970, an earthquake set off another wall of ice, rock and snow that hurtled for 10 miles (16 km) at speeds of up to 174 mph (280 km/h). This time the death toll was 20,000.

AMAZING!

AVALANCHE EXPRESS

In 1910, the Spokane Express, a train bound for Seattle in the United States, got trapped in a blizzard and snow drifts at Wellington station for five days. Then an avalanche rumbled down Windy Mountain. It slammed into the express and a mail train. The carriages were swept into a deep gorge, and 96 passengers and crew were killed.

AVALANCHES AVALANCHAS
VALANGHE LAWINEN

AU-DELÀ DE CETTE LIMITE, VOUS RISQUEZ DE METTRE VOTRE VIE, CELLES DES SAUVETEURS ET DES AUTRES EN DANGER.

PASSING THIS BOUNDARY YOU ENDANGER YOUR LIFE, THE LIFE OF THE OTHERS AND THE RESCUERS'LIVES.

OLTREPASSANDO QUESTO LIMITE METTI IN PERICOLA LA TUA VITA, QUELLA DEGLI ALTRI E DEI SOCCORRITORI.

MAS ALLA DE ESTE LIMITE, CORREN EL RIESGO DE PONER SU VIDA, LA DE LOS OTROS Y DE LOS SALVADORES EN PELIGRO.

ÜBER DIESE GRENZE HINAUS GEFÄHRDEN SIE IHR LEBEN, DAS DER ANDEREN UND DAS DER RETTER.

NO ESCAPE!

We all have a deep-rooted fear of being dragged down into something that we can't escape from. If you get sucked into a bog, swamp, quicksand or a whirlpool, the chances of rescue are slim. What a gruesome way to go!

BOG TERRORS

Bogs and marshes are scary places. Venture off the path and you may find yourself squelching and flailing as you sink into the slime. The bogs of Europe contain dead people that are thousands of years old. Their bodies are often found, perfectly preserved, in these cold, acidic, oxygen-free environments. Many seem to be Iron Age human sacrifices or executed prisoners.

SWAMP KILLER

The real danger from swamps is not so much the terrain as the creatures that live there. The deadliest of all is the mosquito. This insect breeds in wetlands, and some species pass on malaria, a disease that kills between 655,000 and 1.2 million people worldwide each year. That really is a natural disaster.

WHIRLING WATERS

Whirlpool, vortex, maelstrom... All these words describe the spot where powerful tides and currents collide, creating a deadly, spinning wheel of water in seas and straits. Whirlpool currents can reach 23 mph (37 km/h), as around the Moskstraumen eddies in the Norwegian Sea. Fishermen and kayakers must be careful if they want to avoid being pulled down to drown in the seaweed.

AMAZING!

HELP!

Swampy environments make rescue or salvage extremely difficult. In 1996, a DC-9 passenger jet crashed into a deep-water swamp in Florida, with the loss of 110 lives. Access to the crash was extremely hazardous because of the thick vegetation – and the alligators!

QUICKSAND PANIC

When sand is saturated with water, the pressure from one step can turn it into a quivering jelly, called quicksand. If someone sinks in, the more they thrash around, the worse it gets. If it happens to you, here's what to do. Spread out you arms and legs very slowly and try to get on your back. You'll float safely more often than the horror movies let on! The real danger is panic – and of course the incoming tide.

11A ▶

12

DANGER! Quicksand

CATASTROPHIC ACCIDENTS

Gruesome disasters usually strike without warning and have devastating consequences. When the cause of the disaster is human error or design failure, it is doubly tragic – for the catastrophe may have been avoidable.

SINKING OF THE TITANIC

The *Titanic* was the pride of the White Star line – the largest and finest ship on the oceans in 1912. While making its maiden voyage from the English port of Southampton to New York City, with approximately 2,200 passengers and crew on board (the exact figure is not known), the ship struck an iceberg. It sank to the ocean floor. About 1,500 people perished on board or in the freezing waves. The ship was not carrying enough lifeboats for everybody.

FIREBALL

Back in the 1930s, luxurious airships were the fashionable way to travel. They were cylindrical in shape, like big cigars. In 1937, the German airship *Hindenburg* flew from Frankfurt to New Jersey, USA. Attempts to moor the ship to a mast at the Lakehurst Naval Air Station turned into a calamity. A fire broke out and hydrogen gas formed a ferocious ball of fire. The disaster claimed 36 lives.

THE GREAT PLUNGE

Howling winds and fierce storms were battering Scotland's recently constructed Tay Rail Bridge on the evening of 28 December, 1879. It was, at that time, the world's longest bridge, with 85 spans. When the Dundee train steamed over it, the iron girder design failed and collapsed. Locomotive and carriages fell into the dark waters below, killing 75 people.

SPACE TRAGEDY

The take-off of the space shuttle *Challenger* in 1986 impressed the world. Many American school children were watching the live broadcast on television, because the crew included a teacher, Christa McAuliffe. But within just 73 seconds, their joy turned to horror. The spacecraft was breaking up, due to a design flaw. A plume of smoke and debris marked the tragic end of a dream.

DISASTROUS EXPEDITIONS

It takes guts to set off into the unknown and explore the wilderness. Today's explorers may have radio backup and support, but in the old days it was man against nature, one to one. And often it was nature that won!

THE ORDEAL

In 1860, the explorers Robert O'Hara Burke and William John Wills left Melbourne, Australia, to cross the parched heartlands of the country by camel. They succeeded (almost), but the return journey was disastrous. There were deaths, arguments and missed meetings, and a lack of supplies meant they had to eat camel, snakes and seeds that made them ill. Both explorers died (Burke under this tree), and only one team member returned to tell the story.

AN AWFUL PLACE...

In 1910–1912, Robert Falcon Scott led a British expedition to the South Pole. The explorers were brave, but it all went horribly wrong. Their motor sledges were useless and the ponies had to be shot. A Norwegian team, led by Roald Amundsen, reached the Pole just before them. "Great God! This is an awful place..." wrote Scott in his diary. On the return journey, the weather worsened, and they ran short of food and fuel. One man died after cracking his head. Another caught frostbite. Not one of them made it back to base.

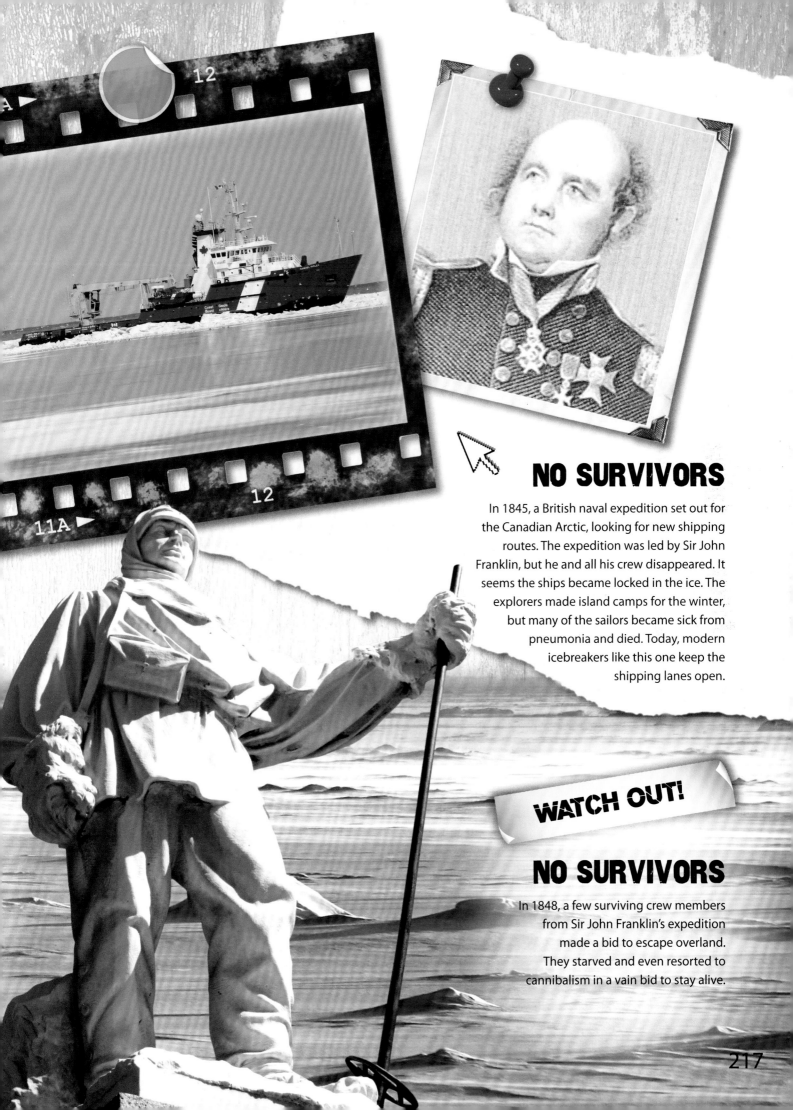

NO SURVIVORS

In 1845, a British naval expedition set out for the Canadian Arctic, looking for new shipping routes. The expedition was led by Sir John Franklin, but he and all his crew disappeared. It seems the ships became locked in the ice. The explorers made island camps for the winter, but many of the sailors became sick from pneumonia and died. Today, modern icebreakers like this one keep the shipping lanes open.

WATCH OUT!

NO SURVIVORS

In 1848, a few surviving crew members from Sir John Franklin's expedition made a bid to escape overland. They starved and even resorted to cannibalism in a vain bid to stay alive.

INDEX

PICTURE CREDITS